What the papers say about Vernon Coleman:

'No thinking person can ignore him.' THE ECOLOGIST

'The calmest voice of reason.' THE OBSERVER

'A godsend.' DAILY TELEGRAPH

'Superstar.' INDEPENDENT ON SUNDAY

'Brilliant!' THE PEOPLE

'Compulsive reading.' THE GUARDIAN

'His message is important.' THE ECONOMIST

'He's the Lone Ranger, Robin Hood and the Equalizer rolled into one.' GLASGOW EVENING TIMES

'The man is a national treasure.' WHAT DOCTORS DON'T TELL YOU

'His advice is optimistic and enthusiastic.' BMJ

'Revered guru of medicine.' NURSING TIMES

'Hard hitting...inimitably forthright.' HULL DAILY MAIL

'Refreshingly forthright.' LIVERPOOL DAILY POST

'It's impossible not to be impressed.' WESTERN DAILY PRESS

'Outspoken and alert.' SUNDAY EXPRESS

'Controversial and devastating.' PUBLISHING NEWS

'Dr Coleman made me think again.' BBC WORLD SERVICE

'Marvellously succinct, refreshingly sensible.' THE SPECTATOR

'Probably one of the most brilliant men alive today.' IRISH TIMES

'Vernon Coleman writes brilliant books.' THE GOOD BOOK GUIDE

'King of the media docs.' THE INDEPENDENT

'Britain's leading medical author.' THE STAR

'Britain's leading health care campaigner.' THE SUN

'Perhaps the best known health writer for the general public in the world today.' THE THERAPIST

'The patient's champion.' BIRMINGHAM POST

'A persuasive writer whose arguments, based on research and experience, are sound.' NURSING STANDARD

'The doctors who dares to speak his mind.' OXFORD MAIL

'He writes lucidly and wittily.' GOOD HOUSEKEEPING

Books by Vernon Coleman include:

The Medicine Men (1975)
Paper Doctors (1976)
Stress Control (1978)
The Home Pharmacy (1980)
Aspirin or Ambulance (1980)
Face Values (1981)
The Good Medicine Guide (1982)
Bodypower (1983)
Thomas Winsden's Cricketing Almanack (1983)
Diary of a Cricket Lover (1984)
Bodysense (1984)
Life Without Tranquillisers (1985)
The Story Of Medicine (1985, 1998)
Mindpower (1986)
Addicts and Addictions (1986)
Dr Vernon Coleman's Guide To Alternative Medicine (1988)
Stress Management Techniques (1988)
Know Yourself (1988)
The Health Scandal (1988)
The 20 Minute Health Check (1989)
Sex For Everyone (1989)
Mind Over Body (1989)
Eat Green Lose Weight (1990)
How To Overcome Toxic Stress (1990)
Why Animal Experiments Must Stop (1991)
The Drugs Myth (1992)
Complete Guide To Sex (1993)
How to Conquer Backache (1993)
How to Conquer Pain (1993)
Betrayal of Trust (1994)
Know Your Drugs (1994, 1997)
Food for Thought (1994, revised edition 2000)
The Traditional Home Doctor (1994)
People Watching (1995)
Relief from IBS (1995)
The Parent's Handbook (1995)
Men in Dresses (1996)
Power over Cancer (1996)
Crossdressing (1996)
How to Conquer Arthritis (1996)
High Blood Pressure (1996)
How To Stop Your Doctor Killing You (1996, revised edition 2003)
Fighting For Animals (1996)
Alice and Other Friends (1996)
Spiritpower (1997)
How To Publish Your Own Book (1999)
How To Relax and Overcome Stress (1999)
Animal Rights – Human Wrongs (1999)
Superbody (1999)

Complete Guide to Life (2000)
Strange But True (2000)
Daily Inspirations (2000)
Stomach Problems: Relief At Last (2001)
How To Overcome Guilt (2001)
How To Live Longer (2001)
Sex (2001)
We Love Cats (2002)
England Our England (2002)
Rogue Nation (2003)
People Push Bottles Up Peaceniks (2003)
The Cats' Own Annual (2003)
Confronting The Global Bully (2004)
Saving England (2004)
Why Everything Is Going To Get Worse Before It Gets Better (2004)
The Secret Lives of Cats (2004)
The Cat Basket (2005)
The Truth They Won't Tell You (And Don't Want You To Know) About The EU (2005)
Living in a Fascist Country (2006)
How To Protect & Preserve Your Freedom, Identity & Privacy (2006)
The Cataholic's Handbook (2006)
Animal Experiments: Simple Truths (2006)
Coleman's Laws (2006)
Secrets of Paris (2007)
Cat Fables (2007)
Too Sexy To Print (2007)
Oil Apocalypse (2007)
Gordon is a Moron (2007)
The OFPIS File (2008)
Cat Tales (2008)
What Happens Next? (2009)
Moneypower (2009)
Bloodless Revolution (2009)
Catoons From Catland (2009)

novels
The Village Cricket Tour (1990)
The Bilbury Chronicles (1992)
Bilbury Grange (1993)
Mrs Caldicot's Cabbage War (1993)
Bilbury Revels (1994)
Deadline (1994)
The Man Who Inherited a Golf Course (1995)
Bilbury Pie (1995)
Bilbury Country (1996)
Second Innings (1999)
Around the Wicket (2000)
It's Never Too Late (2001)
Paris In My Springtime (2002)
Mrs Caldicot's Knickerbocker Glory (2003)

Too Many Clubs And Not Enough Balls (2005)
Tunnel (1980, 2005)
Mr Henry Mulligan (2007)
Bilbury Village (2008)
Bilbury Pudding (2009)

as Edward Vernon
Practice Makes Perfect (1977)
Practise What You Preach (1978)
Getting Into Practice (1979)
Aphrodisiacs – An Owner's Manual (1983)

with Alice
Alice's Diary (1989)
Alice's Adventures (1992)

with Donna Antoinette Coleman
How To Conquer Health Problems Between Ages 50 & 120 (2003)
Health Secrets Doctors Share With Their Families (2005)
Animal Miscellany (2008)

101 Things I Have Learned

Private And Confidential Thoughts On Surviving The Coming Economic, Social And Cultural Chaos

Vernon Coleman

Published by Blue Books, Publishing House, Trinity Place, Barnstaple, Devon EX32 9HG, England.

ISBN: 978-1-899726-17-2

A catalogue record for this book is available from the British Library.

Printed by CPI Antony Rowe

Dedication

To Donna Antoinette with all my love; my haven amidst the turmoil;
my refuge from the storm.

Boring Bit For Lawyers

These days, most books include disclaimers in which the authors apologetically warn readers that they should not rely on any information their books contain, and nor should they follow any of the advice they may find within. The warnings invariably go on to insist that readers who rely on anything in the book they are reading do so at their own risk. These warnings are included because the world is now full of lawyers and litigants who, under the often misguided impression that there might be money to be made, will leap at every opportunity to gouge lolly out of anyone who can be blamed for fate's little tricks. And so, as author and publisher, I feel that I must follow fashion and warn readers that if they act on any of the facts in this book, or decide to follow any of the advice, they do so entirely at their own risk. I advise readers to treat facts with disdain. I recommend that advice and opinions should be disregarded or treated with great suspicion. Any reader who believes the facts in this book, or follows advice the book contains, does so entirely at their own risk. Moreover, I would also like to make it clear that books can be dangerous objects and should not be dropped, thrown or otherwise projected into areas where people or delicate objects might be damaged. In other words, dear reader, drop this book onto your toes and you're on your own.

Preface

These are difficult and challenging times and I believe that things are likely to become considerably worse before they get better. The increasing powers of bureaucrats, and the oppressive nature of the flow of new laws washing onto our shore from the European Union, mean that these are particularly difficult times for those who value their privacy, independence and security. It is no longer possible to rely on traditional sources of help because those whom we pay to protect us and serve us are now largely controlled by, and work for, the bureaucrats. The people we think of as 'them' are all around us. We have to rely upon ourselves.

Over the years I have written scores of books containing information and advice on medical, social and financial matters. It seemed to me a good time to produce a précis of some of the most pertinent advice in a short survival handbook. And this is that book. Of all the books I have written this is probably the most immediately practical. It is an abstract of some of the information in my other books, a brief analysis of how I believe things are likely to change in the foreseeable future and a summary of things I've learned about surviving in an increasingly hostile environment. (The background information behind the advice in this book appears in my original books. There's a list at the front of this book and short descriptions of some at the back.)

Government regulations mean that in some countries it is probably illegal for me to offer you advice in many areas of life (such as finance). If it isn't now then it could be soon. So I'm not going to offer you any specific advice at all. What follows is a précis of what I have learned, and a short analysis of how the things I have learned can be applied to life in the future. Experiences, mistakes and insights are of little use until you learn from them and take advantage of them.

'Of all writings I love only that which is written with blood,' wrote Frederick Nietzsche, who wrote with nothing else. 'Write with blood: and you will discover that blood is spirit.'

Vernon Coleman, Bilbury, Devon, October 2009

101 Things I Have Learned

1. I have learned that if I am receiving treatment for an existing disease and I develop new symptoms then, until proved otherwise, I should assume that the new symptoms are caused by the treatment I am receiving.

This is Coleman's First Law of Medicine and knowing it, and remembering it, could save your life.

Doctors are notoriously reluctant to admit that the treatments they recommend can do harm. There are several reasons for this. First, they often simply don't know how dangerous drugs can be (doctors rarely bother to read drug company information sheets). Second, they are frightened of being sued. (Doctors fear that if they admit that their treatment made someone ill they will receive a letter from a lawyer. Like most people they don't like letters from lawyers.) And finally, born of stubbornness and pride, there is a natural human unwillingness to admit responsibility for something that has gone wrong. This brand of unwillingness is unusually well developed among doctors who are encouraged to think of themselves as godlike by many of their more passive patients. Admitting to having made someone ill reminds doctors that they are mortal and fallible.

Because doctors almost never admit that the drugs they have prescribed might have caused unpleasant or dangerous side effects very few incidences of drug–induced illness are reported to the official watchdogs and this enables doctors and drug companies to claim that prescription drugs are safe. (The word 'safe' is, of course, relative. Even though the number of reported side effects is absurdly low, doctors are now officially one of the top four causes of death and serious injury in the world. They share the top four spots with cancer, heart disease and stroke.)

The truth is that side effects are far commoner than most people (including doctors) think. Four out of every ten patients who take a prescription drug will develop side effects. Some side effects will be mild and others will be unpleasant but many will be dangerous and potentially life–threatening. And one in six patients in hospital are there because they've been made ill by a doctor.

2. I have learned that the best way to beat the financial markets is to make geopolitical predictions and to then invest accordingly.

Most investors (and most investment advisers) do not do this. This may be because they can't or because they prefer to look at the trees rather than study the woods. In my experience, it always pays to look out for new trends and big themes. For example, investors who are aware of the problem of peak oil are well placed to take advantage of the coming rise in oil prices. If there were an efficient way to invest, using computer power, the investment bankers would own all the money. But although they have more than they deserve they don't have all the money – so there is no efficient way to invest. Computers cannot yet predict movements in the financial markets. The private investor who uses his intelligence, and watches and listens, is more likely to be successful than the professional investor who is constrained by corporate requirements, bonus driven short–termism, unbridled greed and a dangerous lack of common sense. (The world's investment bankers do have a lot of money. But they acquire it through trickery, deceit and crookery rather than through skills, knowledge or intelligence.)

The most important skill for any investor is, in my view, the ability to differentiate between relevant and irrelevant news. To be successful it is essential to be able to dismiss investment or geopolitical 'noise' and to focus on crucial bits and pieces of information.

It is, of course, also essential to be able to interpret the information you have selected and to use that information to help you draw conclusions. And it isn't information that matters in the world of investing: it is knowing how other people will respond to the available information.

I have also learned to be patient with winners and impatient with losers. Remember: it is possible to be very successful by being right 30% of the time, as long as you hold your winners and sell your losers. I have learned not to expect a chosen investment to rise immediately after I've bought it. You might have to wait a while for the rest of the market to realise that you're a genius and that they want to make the same investment decision that you've made. Investing is like tennis and golf. At the top level the winners are the ones who make the fewest mistakes. (I have no qualifications as an investment adviser but in support of my comments about investing I should, perhaps, point out that according to a rough and quite unaudited assessment, I appear to have made an average annual capital gain of around 17% for each of the years from 2000 to 2009 on my personal investment portfolio (excluding dividends and interest). I have described my investment principles in detail in my book *Moneypower*.)

I have learned that it is vital to know your weaknesses as an investor. Do you tend to react too much to small items of news? Do you listen too much to what other people say? Are you afraid of losing money? Are you afraid of making money? Do you feel guilty about having money? Until you know yourself, you will not make a competent investor. If you are to be a successful investor you must know what you want from your investments. And you must know what you are prepared to risk in order to get what you want. No one knows as well as you do what risks you are prepared to take. No one else knows what makes you comfortable. This philosophy can be applied to all aspects of life. So, just as you are the best medical adviser you will ever have so, too, you are also the best financial adviser you will ever have.

I have learned that if you spot an investment bandwagon you've missed it. If other people are climbing on then you should be climbing off. If you buy an investment which everyone else agrees is worth buying then you are probably paying too much. This is true for every investment you can think of – including bonds, shares and property.

The key to successful investing is to look at geopolitical issues, to spot global trends and to understand their importance. Successful investing involves anticipating change, not reacting to it. And remember: big investment opportunities are rare. When you spot one, and you are sure, you have to seize it with both hands.

You should always be able to explain your investments to anyone in a few simple sentences. If you buy a share, or put money into an investment trust or fund, you should be able to summarise your reasons in sentences that anyone could understand. And you need to be able to explain why you are continuing to hold this investment on a regular basis – particularly if anything changes.

When my book *Oil Apocalypse* was published it and I were treated to a barrage of sceptical criticism. My critics were, presumably, happy to ignore the investment advice in the book. I took my own advice and, believing, that the oil price would rise I bought oil.

It isn't easy to purchase a barrel of oil. It's heavy and messy. And I suspect the bank wouldn't look on me kindly if I ask them to let me store a few barrels of oil in their vault. But you can, of course, buy oil company shares. Big oil companies tend to do well when the price of oil goes up. They also pay handsome dividends. I also bought shares in smaller, more risky oil companies. Independent oil producers and explorers may be 'dangerous' but if the oil price rockets and they have oil to sell then their share price will rocket too. And I bought oil service companies – the companies providing oil rigs and other equipment to oil explorers and to companies drilling for oil. Despite the economic crisis the shares have done very nicely, thank you. I believe that holding such shares will, at the very least, give me a hedge against the price rise. As the cost of heating my home, and filling my petrol tank rises, so will my investment in oil shares.

3. I have learned not to trust the experts.

When I was young I was often advised that I should never do anything new or imaginative without first consulting the experts. When I was young I thought this was good advice. I have, however, learned to be constantly sceptical about the advice I receive from professionals. Today, all professions are run by a small group of establishment figures. These are usually wealthy and ambitious individuals who have acquired power over their professions by taking on administrative and management work that no one else is much interested in. They speak for, and make decisions on behalf of, thousands of their fellow professionals. This is particularly true of medicine and the law. It isn't a new phenomenon.

When he wrote *An Inquiry into the Nature and Causes of the Wealth of Nations* (a book now better known as *Wealth of Nations*) Adam Smith wrote: 'People of the same trade seldom meet together, even for merriment or diversion, but the conversation ends in a conspiracy against the public.' I don't know whether Smith regarded doctors and lawyers as 'trade' in 1776. But both medicine and the law are now most certainly 'trades'. As I wrote in *The Medicine Men* in 1975, a profession which takes its instructions from an industry is no more than a trade. Lawyers now advertise their services alongside plumbers, electricians and double glazing specialists.

Patients used to hand over their health (and their lives) to their doctors – without ever questioning what was happening to them. Today, that is a dangerous way to live. Patients who take an interest in their own health (and in the investigations and treatments that are recommended for them) may sometimes feel that the doctors and nurses who are looking after them regard them as a nuisance. But all the evidence shows clearly that such patients get better quicker, suffer fewer unpleasant side effects and live longer than patients who simply lie back passively and allow the professionals to take over.

If your doctor wants you to take a drug (and all pills, tablets, capsules, medicines, potions and so on are drugs) make sure you know what to expect. If your doctor wants you to have surgery then make sure that you know what the surgery entails, what the possible consequences might be and what the alternatives are. Two really good questions to ask your doctor are: 'Would you have this operation if you were me?' and 'Would you recommend this operation to someone in your close family?'

Learn as much as you can about any disorder from which you suffer. And learn about all the possible types of treatment available. Patients who know more about their condition than their doctors invariably do better than patients who know nothing and put all their trust in their medical advisers.

I am similarly sceptical about investment advisers. Traditional investment rules all rely on hindsight. In practice, it is forecasting skills which really count. Charts of the past can be useful but they are a shaky basis upon which to base plans.

I think it is important not to overestimate the intelligence of the investment professionals. For example, the so-called 'credit–crunch' which devastated the financial markets (and the share prices of banks) from 2007 onwards affected Britain because so many leading bankers behaved like idiots and bought packages of mortgage debt without, apparently, having asked fairly fundamental questions about the security of the assets they were buying. People who borrowed huge amounts of money which they had no chance of ever paying back were reckless. But it was the hubris of bankers which led directly to serious losses for investors and real problems for millions.

The collapse of Long Term Capital Management (LTCM) in 1998 proved that clever people with lots of computers are not very good at managing, or even keeping, money. LTCM was run by people who had big brains and Nobel prizes. It was supposed to be the Titanic of investment funds. But, like the Titanic, it ran into serious trouble. Hubris led LTCM onto the iceberg of the Russian Government defaulting on sovereign debt. If the American Government hadn't bailed LTCM out (or, rather, strong–armed investment banks to take over its positions) LTCM would have gone bankrupt with disastrous results.

And what an indictment it is of investment managers that they all have to put on their advertisements 'Past performance is no guarantee or indicator of future performance.' I wonder how many cars would be sold if their dealers had to put that sort of slogan on all their dashboards. How many patients would visit a doctor who warned all his patients that 'past performance was no guarantee or indicator of future performance'.

The entire financial industry exists to sell things and to make money out of you. If you don't understand – and remember this – you will be cheated, tricked and conned.

I have learned that when I am among investment professionals I am the only person interested in making money for me. Everyone else is interested in making money from me. You will look after your money better than anyone else will. Investing isn't difficult. Most of the people who do it for a living are half–wits.

If you're saving money you need to know why. And you need to know what your needs are (and are likely to become) and what you are prepared to do to satisfy those needs. You need a strategy. Amazingly few people understand money management (which, although it isn't taught in our schools, is one of the most important skills anyone can have). Most people think they can trust the experts; they think that money management is boring, too complex or beneath them. They think that you need years of training in order to understand shares, bonds and money markets. None of this is true. Most spectacularly successful investors have never had any proper or orthodox training. And if you do decide to manage your own money you will have one huge advantage over everyone else: you will always care more about your money than anyone else will.

Finally, never take investment advice from anyone who isn't a self–made millionaire and/or considerably richer than you are. What does the guy in your local bank know about investments? If he is so good why isn't he rich, rather than sitting behind a desk telling you what to do with your money?

4. I have learned that there is no point in my having medical tests done unless the results of those tests will affect my treatment.

This is Coleman's Second Law of Medicine, and since even seemingly simple tests can sometimes be far more hazardous than doctors are usually prepared to admit, this law, like the first, may prove life—saving.

If your doctor wants you to have tests done ask him how the results will affect your treatment. If the results of the tests won't affect the treatment you receive (and aren't needed as a baseline against which to compare future tests) then the tests aren't worth having.

Tests and investigations are often regarded (by both doctors and patients) as being harmless. They aren't. There is no such thing as minor surgery and even taking blood is an operation. There are dangers inherent in every test that is performed. And there is, in addition, the danger that the result will be wrong and that your doctors will treat the faulty test rather than treating you. Thousands of healthy people have died from treatments they never needed. (If a surgeon recommends surgery that won't save your life ask yourself this one question: can I live with the problem and without the surgery? And remember: no surgery is free of risks.)

5. I have learned that party politicians can only be trusted to be untrustworthy.

I have learned to expect nothing from them but allegiance to their parties and their own self—centred interests. I have learned to make no plans which depend upon their integrity or reliability.

Modern politicians are self—serving; they are professional liars whose sole interest lies in preserving their own careers and the status and wealth that they have grown accustomed to. I believe that it is invariably safe to assume that everything politicians say is a lie, that every promise they make will be broken and that all their grandiose schemes will end in failure. Occasional truths and successes will not affect the overall effectiveness of this attitude.

We must plan our lives on the basis that nothing politicians tell us can be trusted. This is not cynicism or pessimism. It is pragmatism.

And so, for example, I have learned never, never, never to invest on the basis of a politician's promise. Politicians talk a great deal about improving infrastructure, and they boast about improving spending on health care and education. But their promises are easily abandoned. (And now that we have been impoverished by incompetent politicians and thieving bankers the future will be ever bleaker.) Companies which adapt their plans to fit in with potentially profitable opportunities which might result from political changes are taking huge chances. I would never invest in a company which will supposedly benefit from any government decision.

The bottom line is that governments and bureaucrats will always make a far greater mess of things than ever seemed possible. And they will keep on making a mess for longer than seemed possible, too. Whatever problems the future holds for the world, governments everywhere will mess up everything that can be messed up and they will make everything worse.

Our public sector is bloated, self–indulgent and irredeemably corrupt. Where there is an opportunity to waste they will find it in an instant and proceed to take advantage of the opportunity for longer than is decently possible. (A recent Government report concluded, apparently without whimsy, that private companies can, on average, do any job performed by a Government department for two thirds of the cost. Naturally, there are no plans to do anything about this.)

It is safe to rely on the stupidity and incompetence and dishonesty of politicians. They will not do sensible things (however simple) to correct substantial threats to the economy but can be relied upon to lie, cheat and make things worse in their efforts to preserve their own miserable careers.

6. I have learned that the oil is running out.

I simply do not believe the optimistic ostriches who insist that everything is going to be fine and that oil companies will manage to find new oil fields when the old ones run out.

It was oil which took us out of the Steam Age. And nothing in history has changed our lives in the way that oil has done.

But now the oil is running out and, whether the politicians and the bureaucrats like it or not, our civilisation will have to change. (I have described some of the ways in which our world must change in my book *Oil Apocalypse*.)

Having oil has changed our world. Having oil changed the way our economy grew, it changed the way we move about the planet, it changed the way our factories operate, it changed the way we live and the food we eat. Oil revolutionised our lives.

And now the oil is running out.

Our governments will make no useful plans to deal with the changes which must come. And so we must make our own plans. We must prepare ourselves, mentally and physically, for a different world. We must learn to be more self–sufficient and we must prepare ourselves for a world in which oil becomes steadily but remorselessly increasingly expensive and difficult to get hold of.

There is much we can do. In many ways the world may well prove to be a calmer, more peaceful and more comfortable place without oil.

But first we must learn to accept that the oil is running out.

7. I have learned that when I am investing with the aim of preserving my savings, or helping them grow, I should not invest in 'state of the art' technology.

The investors who put money into the early railroads or airline companies were (to say the least) usually disappointed with their returns. Investing in 'new' things (such as dot.com companies) can be just as frustrating, disappointing and expensive now as it was then.

When global warming became 'trendy' people started looking at alternative forms of energy as an investment possibility. Sadly, many investments in alternative energy proved disappointing because although the theory was fine the companies had no realistic chance of making a profit. In some cases there was no real demand for their products. In other cases the products simply weren't terribly good.

As the oil and gas run out, and the energy crisis develops, you might think it would be wise to invest in alternatives – companies making windmills or solar panels, for example.

But I haven't invested in alternative technologies (such as wind or solar power) for two reasons.

First, my personal feeling is that companies in these areas have been overbought and are overpriced. A number of investors have already pushed up the prices of companies in this area. There simply aren't many bargains around any more.

Second, I don't think any government on the planet is taking these alternatives seriously and I think these companies will, therefore, struggle to bloom. I just don't believe that any government is going to do the sensible thing and put money and effort into encouraging alternative forms of energy. When governments finally realise that they should have encouraged these companies it will be too late – the governments won't have any money left to invest.

8. I have learned to have faith in gold and silver.

Many investment advisors, banks and others who claim to know about these things sneer at gold as an investment.

'It doesn't pay any interest and you have to pay to store it,' is the usual argument against investing in gold.

These investors claim that gold is of interest only as a historical relic. And as a metal for making jewellery.

But I believe that they are wrong.

Gold used to be the basis upon which most currencies were based. People used to pay one another in gold coins. When paper currency replaced gold coins (because it was thought to be more practical to carry around a bundle of fivers than a bag of gold sovereigns) governments only issued as much paper currency as matched the gold they held in their vaults.

That was the deal upon which citizens accepted paper money. The bank note was a piece of paper which their government issued in lieu of gold. And the value of all the bits of paper the government issued never exceeded the value of the gold the government held in its vault. A citizen could take a bank note along to the Bank and exchange it for gold. People liked that. It made them feel comfortable.

This was important because as well as being a medium for buying and selling everyday 'things', and providing a unit by which such deals could be priced, money also had to act as a store of value.

Even since the first man started buying and selling cows and baskets of wheat, society has needed a way for people to save their money safely. Savings, and wealth, provide some sort of insurance against the bad days that come. If you have some money stored then you can buy grain if a freak storm destroys your own crops.

And people have always wanted to know that the money they saved would hold its value.

Before inflation became an accepted (and expected) way of life, a gold coin or a small gold bar would be just as valuable when you took it out of its hiding place as it had been when you put it in there.

Gold is valuable because it remains in limited supply. All the gold ever mined would fit into a 20 yard cube. And despite the fact that there are numerous exploration companies in existence there just doesn't seem to be much more gold waiting to be discovered.

Gold has always been a good hedge against inflation. The Government can print money but it can't manufacture gold. And gold has always held its value. 'You have to choose (as a voter) between trusting the natural stability of gold and the honest and intelligence of members of government,' wrote George Bernard Shaw. 'And with due respect to those gentlemen, I advise you, as long as the capitalist system lasts, to vote for gold.' I think he was right.

Shares in gold mining companies usually rise faster than the price of the metal alone. When the price rises the costs of getting the metal out of the ground stays much the same so the profit goes up. (The danger, of course, is that the cost of oil will make the cost of extracting the gold much, much higher.)

Buying gold is easy. (There is no real point in buying gold jewellery as an investment. Gold jewellery prices are much higher than the cost of the gold because of the labour involved in making and selling jewellery.) Gold coins such as krugerrands and sovereigns are fairly easy to buy from dealers. Some small jewellery shops sell gold coins.

I have a suspicion that the price of gold may soar. I believe it will, at least, retain its value in increasingly difficult times. I look upon buying gold as an insurance plan. If politicians around the globe provide us with exemplary leadership and the world manages perfectly well without oil (an unlikely prospect, it seems to me) then buying gold is probably unnecessary. But whenever I buy insurance I always hope that the premium will be wasted.

I have learned that if gold goes up in value then silver will probably follow.

Silver has a long history as a currency. The French word for money is 'argent' which comes from the Latin word argentum which means silver. The currency of India is the rupee. The word comes from a Sanskrit word for silver or a silver coin. Gold was usually used for large financial transactions but most countries in the world used silver for smaller denomination coins. In America silver dimes and quarters were made of 90% silver up until 1965.

Today silver is still indispensable to many industries. It is very strong but also extremely malleable. It has the highest thermal conductivity of all metals, the highest electrical conductivity and the best optical reflectivity too. It can put up with extremes of temperature without changing its properties. It even has powerful qualities as a disinfectant. It is used to prevent bacterial infections in burn victims and many wound dressings incorporate a layer of fabric which contains silver to prevent secondary infections developing. Silver is used in mobile telephones, washing machines, television sets, toasters, mirrors, cameras, photography, many medical devices, computer keyboards and a vast variety of other gadgets. Industrial demand for silver is currently rising at around 6% a year. And, of course, most of the silver used in industry cannot be recycled.

In the year 1900 there were 12 billion ounces of silver in the world. By 1990, the amount of silver had been reduced to 2.2 billion ounces. Today there are said to be around 300 million ounces of above ground refined silver left in existence. An astonishing 95% of the silver ever mined has been consumed by the photography, medical, defence, electronic and technology industries. The silver that has gone is gone for ever.

Why hasn't the price rocketed? Simple: the gap between demand and supply has been filled from official government stockpiles. Governments have been as keen to get rid of silver as they have been to dump their gold supplies.

9. I have learned that there is a single food that causes as many deaths and as much illness as tobacco.

It is a food which has been proven time and time again to cause cancer of the breast, cancer of the prostate, cancer of the bowel, many other types of cancer and numerous other disorders including asthma, heart disease, constipation, high blood pressure, osteoporosis and rheumatoid arthritis. It is a food which most people eat at least once every day. And it is a food which governments know is potentially lethal but which they support (with subsidies) and actively promote.

The truth about this deadly food is suppressed for purely commercial reasons. Governments (and the medical profession) say nothing because the people selling the food have too much power and too much money.

The name of the food is meat.

It is, I believe, the fat in meat which is the most significant cause of cancer. The fat in meat isn't just the white stuff that is easy to cut off. The fat is spread throughout the meat and is invisible to the naked eye.

The fat in meat is particularly likely to cause cancer because the carcinogenic chemicals fed to animals accumulate in the animal's fatty tissues. When the fatty meat is eaten the carcinogenic chemicals easily accumulate in the parts of the human body with the most fat. Breast cancer is a particular risk because breast tissue contains a considerable amount of fatty tissue. The incidence of breast cancer is rocketing (as are so many other cancers) because of chemical toxins in the fatty meat we eat. Clear scientific evidence shows that women who eat lots of fat, and/or eat lots of meat, are more likely to get breast cancer. It really is that simple. The incidence of breast cancer among Japanese women was low when they ate a traditional Japanese diet (which contains very little meat). When Japanese women started eating fatty hamburgers (food which I long ago christened harmburgers) the incidence of breast cancer rocketed.

There is plenty of evidence proving that meat causes cancer (there are summaries of 26 scientific papers relating meat to cancer in my book *Food for Thought*) but, despite this, there are many doctors, dieticians and nutritionists around who still don't seem to understand the importance of this link. Despite the firm evidence showing that meat causes cancer the majority of hospitals still serve their patients (and staff) meals which are built around meat. We think it strange that just a relatively few years ago patients and staff in hospitals were allowed to smoke on the wards but in a few years time our descendants will surely regard it as just as odd that hospitals should have served meat to people entrusted to their care. In my view, any nutritionist, dietician, cookery writer or chef who advocates eating meat should be doing something else for a living. I believe it is as absurd and as indefensible for a chef, nutritionist or dietician to recommend eating meat as part of a healthy diet as it would be for a doctor to recommend smoking as part of a healthy lifestyle.

The list of diseases known to be associated with meat, or commoner among meat eaters, looks like the index of a medical textbook. Anaemia, appendicitis, arthritis, breast cancer, cancer of the colon, cancer of the prostate, constipation, diabetes, gall stones, gout, high blood pressure, indigestion, obesity, piles, strokes and varicose veins are just some of the well–known disorders which are more likely to affect meat eaters than vegetarians.

There is too, the problem of the adrenalin in meat. When animals are killed they are inevitably terrified. They have a good deal of adrenalin running through their veins. When the animal is eaten the person who eats the animal consumes that adrenalin. What are the consequences of this? No one knows.

To all these hazards must be added the fact that if you eat meat you will be consuming any hormones, drugs and other chemicals which may have been fed to the animals before they were killed.

No one knows precisely what effect eating the hormones in meat is likely to have on your health. But the risk is there and I think it's a big one.

And there are other hazards. Some farmers use tranquillisers to keep animals calm. Others routinely use antibiotics so that their animals do not develop infections – and to boost the rate at which they put on weight. In America over half of all antibiotics are fed to animals, and I don't think it is any coincidence that the percentage of staphylococci infections resistant to penicillin has risen dramatically since farmers started doing this. Animals which are lucky enough to spend some of their time out of doors eating grass will often eat grass which has been sprayed with all sorts of toxic and carcinogenic chemicals.

If you care one jot about your health then the very best thing you can do is to give up eating meat. Giving up meat and eating a vegetarian diet will have as dramatic an effect on your health as not smoking.

10. I have learned that it is vital to be a holistic patient.

A truly holistic approach to staying healthy and treating illness depends upon using a wide range of possible remedies; treating the patient's signs and symptoms (rather than his test results) and combining all types of alternative and orthodox medicine.

There are very few truly holistic practitioners around. Doctors often talk about holistic medicine. So do alternative practitioners. But most of them don't have the foggiest idea what it really means. Ford dealers tend to sell Fords; acupuncturists tend to offer acupuncture; herbalists tend to offer herbal remedies; and medical doctors tend to prescribe pills and surgery.

There is, however, nothing at all to stop you being a holistic patient. For example, if your doctor tells you that you need surgery ask him how quickly you need to make a decision – and then use that time to make sure that you assess all the alternative possible options.

When you are trying to choose between orthodox medicine, acupuncture, homeopathy, osteopathy or whatever make a list of all the advantages and disadvantages of every available type of therapy – and every available practitioner. Look at the claims and the potential side effects of each therapy and ask each practitioner to tell you where you can find out more. Use books to educate yourself about the possibilities, advantages and hazards. Never forget that you are unique – and that your condition requires a unique solution.

As a holistic patient you will have to be prepared to stand your ground against health care professionals who will regard your preference for a holistic approach as bizarre.

Many orthodox practitioners are still likely to dismiss alternative or complementary medicine out of hand. If a treatment doesn't involve drugs, surgery or radiotherapy then it's quackery, according to many doctors. (Curiously, young doctors are more likely to be sceptical about alternative medicine than older ones. It seems that the drug industry has, in recent years, improved its effectiveness at increasing scepticism about non–orthodox remedies.)

11. I have learned the importance of being able to say 'No'.

Do you often end up doing things that you don't want to do – simply because you didn't like to say 'No' when you were asked? Have you ever agreed to give a speech, attend a dinner or luncheon, chair a meeting or act as a secretary for a volunteer group? And have you ever subsequently regretted saying 'Yes'?

Life is too short to waste time in such a way.

If you spend too much of your life doing things you don't want to do then you will be losing time and the freedom to spend your life in the way you want to spend it.

We all like to be liked and saying 'Yes' is much more likely to attract approval and a smile from the person doing the asking than is saying 'No'.

We say 'Yes' because we know that the other person will probably feel disappointed or let down if we say 'No'. And we say 'Yes' (when we would really much rather say 'No') when we are not clear enough about our priorities and are, consequently, prepared to let other people decide what we do with our time. It is often easy to forget that saying 'Yes' to a simple sounding request may commit you to a time and energy sapping exercise.

Saying 'No' doesn't have to mean that you annoy people or upset them. Practice saying 'No' nicely and you will find that you can avoid wasting your life doing things you really don't want to do.

Here are some practical tips:

1. Don't be defensive. You have no reason to feel guilty for saying 'No'. Don't begin by apologising.

2. Don't give excuses. If you give excuses you are likely to end up saying 'Yes' when you really mean to say 'No'. For example, if you are invited to speak at a meeting which is being held next Tuesday evening and you say you can't manage that evening because you already have another commitment there is a danger that the person inviting you will suggest another date 'which will be more convenient to you'. At this point you are backed into a corner. And it will be difficult to get out of giving the speech without being rude.

3. Begin your reply by flattering the person who is inviting you to do something. Tell them that you are honoured and flattered by the invitation.

4. Look the person who is inviting you straight in the eye when you reply. This will help you dominate the conversation and ensure that it goes in the way you want it to go. If you look down and avoid eye contact (a natural reaction when you feel guilty or embarrassed) you will be behaving in a 'passive' way. When you behave in a 'passive' way the other person will automatically become more 'aggressive' and 'dominant'.

5. Give a solid reason for not saying 'Yes' – a reason which it will be difficult to oppose or discount. It is even better if you say something which it will

be impossible for the person inviting you to try to push aside without seeming to be rude or thoughtless. If asked to give a speech you don't want to give you can, for example, say: 'From experience I know that this is not something I am good at and so I must say 'No'. But I am flattered that you have asked me.'

Every time you say 'Yes' it should be because you are doing something you want to do, or feel that you can do well, and not because you are frightened to say 'No'.

12. I have learned not to trust anything anyone promises about pensions.

Anyone who is relying on a promised or expected pension that they do not themselves control should beware. As our economy struggles to cope with the huge debts which have been accumulated, and as the peak oil crisis unfolds, many companies will collapse – and their pension plans will collapse with them. Governments will not be able to step into the breach. Indeed, many governments will not be able to meet their responsibilities to their own pensioners. Civil servants, like corporate employees, will find that the pensions they had expected simply aren't available.

As the years go by an increasing number of pensioners will find that the money they thought they would receive when they retired simply isn't there. European Union legislation, and Government intervention, will damage pension funds and result in shrinking pensions.

I believe that the wisest course is to take control of your pension yourself and, if possible, to manage your own investments. Safest of all, perhaps, will be those individuals who save their money, put it into a safe place, but do not confine it to a pension fund.

13. I have learned that if I am receiving medical treatment that doesn't work then I should consider the possibility that the diagnosis might be wrong.

This is particularly true when several treatments have been tried without producing any improvement.

Doctors pay far too much attention to high technology equipment these days. As a result they are often frighteningly bad at making diagnoses. Numerous studies have shown that vast numbers of patients die without ever having been properly diagnosed. One study, using post–mortem examinations to check the cause of death, showed that less than 20% of patients who die have been accurately diagnosed. Even significant, common disorders – such as heart attacks – are often missed. In this survey it was clear that many of the patients would have survived if they had been accurately diagnosed.

I have learned, therefore, never be afraid to ask for a second opinion.

It may be your life that is at stake. Telling your doctor that you want a second opinion will probably take a great deal of courage. Many doctors are sensitive creatures – they may show their hurt if their all–knowingness is questioned. But just remember that the stakes are high.

And, if there is time, don't be afraid to check out the past record of the doctor who is going to treat you. One surgeon working in a hospital may have a survival rate which is twice as good as another surgeon working in the same hospital. If you allow the less competent surgeon to operate on you then your chances of walking out of the hospital may be halved. Those are odds you cannot and should not ignore.

14. I have learned that it is always a good idea to know the 'bottom line'.

If you are contemplating a new business venture, or making a new investment, knowing the bottom line will enable you to make an accurate judgement about whether or not to go ahead.

Always work out the worst case scenario. And give yourself an exit strategy.

Knowing the bottom line will reduce the chances of you panicking. And you must never panic in a crisis. If you panic you will make the wrong decisions. The best way to avoid panicking is to make sure that you don't put yourself in a position where you are ever going to feel uncomfortable or under pressure.

If you are going to take risks successfully you need to be able to assess the bottom line with some degree of accuracy. Only when you know the bottom line will you be able comfortably to take chances that you might otherwise avoid.

Constantly ask yourself: 'What is the worst that can happen?' 'What will/could happen if I do/don't do this?'

You may be surprised to discover that there are not many risks which can make the sky fall in or stop the world going round.

15. I have learned that recycling projects run by local authorities are a nonsense.

Millions of people separate their yoghurt cartons from their cereal packets and their baked bean tins from their old birthday cards and their beer bottles from their newspapers. They then spend time putting these items into separate collecting bins.

Most of them believe that by sorting and recycling their waste they are helping to save the planet. Sadly, they are not.

Much of the material sorted and prepared for recycling simply ends up in landfill sites. I have little doubt that preparing and sorting waste, and then disposing of it, uses up more energy than simply dumping the stuff in suitable landfill sites. We deal with our waste in an unproductive and expensive way because of useless and damaging legislation forced upon us by the European Union.

It would, of course, be far more helpful to force manufacturers and retailers to wrap their products in less packaging.

16. I have learned that the value of soft commodities (corn, wheat, soya, coffee and other crops grown in fields) is likely to keep rising in the medium and long–term.

(I have no idea what is likely to happen in the short–term. Investing for periods of days or weeks is not investing, it is gambling.)

The world's population is growing and people in China and India are no longer content to live on a bowl of rice and beans a day. The demand for meat is putting pressure on agricultural commodities because animals have to be fed.

Other problems mean that prices will probably continue to rise.

First, global warming (whatever the cause) is not good for agriculture. Crops get damaged by drought and damaged by storms. Second, there is a growing global water shortage. Crops need water. Less water will probably mean fewer crops. Third, the mad and indefensible enthusiasm for ethanol as an alternative fuel means that many of the crops sold are being used to enable American motorists to ignore the problems of peak oil. Crops grown and sold as food are bound to get more expensive.

17. I have learned that the best, and safest, way to pay for anything is to use cash and to use credit and debit cards as little as possible.

When I stand in a queue at the newsagents I am constantly surprised by the number of people using plastic to buy one magazine or one notebook. Don't these people have banks with hole–in–the wall cash dispensers?

Using plastic is unwise for two reasons. First, the more you use your cards the more you are likely to end up having your identity stolen. And that's not funny. Second, if you use cards for all your purchases you will lose track of your spending. If you have to go and get the cash out of the bank then you'll know just how fast your money is disappearing. It's much easier to keep control of your spending if you use cash. Third, if you use plastic then anyone following you can easily see where you are. If someone has access to the credit card company's computers they will easily spot that you're on holiday in Brighton and not at your flat in Leeds. This sort of information is quite useful for burglars.

If you are worried about carrying enough cash just split it between two or three wallets. Make sure that the wallet you use in shops only contains a modest amount of cash. Keep the rest of your cash in inside pockets or in a money belt or money pouch of some kind.

And carry what I call a 'mugger's wallet with you. (A mugger's wallet is simply an old wallet which contains a few notes, and a few bits of useless plastic which look like credit cards but aren't. If a mugger demands your wallet, this is the one you hand over.)

18. I have learned that identity theft is the fastest growing criminal industry in the world but that there are a number of things I can do to protect my identity.

First, if a bank or other institution demands to see your passport, driving licence, birth certificate or gas bill then you should do exactly that: let them see it. And then take it away again. Here it is. See it? Whoosh. Now it's gone. Don't let them take a copy. I have done this many times. Petty officials usually complain. But I tell them to check with their compliance officer who will, once he or she has checked the rules, tell them that I'm right. You can do this with solicitors and other professionals too. For most purposes, all these people have to do is to confirm that you are who you say you are. They do not always have the right to copy your confidential information and put it into their system for some half–wit to lose. There are rules requiring institutions and individuals to make sure that you are who you say you are. But that's all. (There are, inevitably some exceptions. For example, employment legislation may give employers a right to demand copies.)

It's up to you whether you do this or not, of course, but if you do not look after your documents then within a few years there will be dozens of copies of your valuable identity documents floating around out of your control. You may think that worrying about this is slightly paranoid but identity theft is now the fastest growing criminal activity in the country. On the rare occasions when copies are needed (as, for example, when dealing with an institution at a distance) I write on the photocopy the date and a note to say that the copy is for the use of that institution only. This makes it impossible for the copy to be used by anyone else for any other purpose.

Second, insist that any private documents which you are required to send are returned to you by private courier (or, at the very least, by special delivery). It may help if you tell the person at the other end that they will be responsible if the documents are lost. Do this, for example, if you have to send your driving licence to a police force to be endorsed. People in authority hate being told that they will be held responsible for anything. And, in general, what they hate is usually good for you.

Incidentally, I was recently told by an estate agent that they would not act for me unless I allowed them to take copies of a variety of private documents. I was told that it would be against the law for me to refuse to allow them to do this. I refused. They sold a house for me. No one has yet been arrested and the sun still comes up every morning.

I have learned to protect my privacy. Once you've lost it, it's a devil of a game to get it back. Indeed, under some circumstances it may be impossible to recover. But you do have to be aware and wary. For example, it is widely believed that by dialling 141 before the number you dial it is possible to protect your telephone identity from the person or company you are calling. Sadly, this is not always the case. All Government agencies can, of course, identify you. And so can a growing number of private companies who use equipment, which may or may not be legal, to break the code and identify your number.

There are, these days, vast numbers of bureaucrats and officials demanding personal information. Whenever I can legally avoid giving them the information they demand, I do so. It's usually easier than you might think. Neither the Government nor my bank knows where I live. And why should they?

19. I have learned that medical screening examinations and check–ups are more profitable for doctors than for patients.

I have been a stern critic of screening examinations and check–ups for several decades and have, in the distant past, pointed out that well–known (and extremely profitable) forms of testing such as the cervical smear, the breast mammogram and the prostate specific antigen test for prostate cancer may, over the years, have done more harm than good. Naturally, my criticisms have been met with a barrage of angry and very defensive comments from doctors who earn their living providing screening tests and from companies which make money out of producing screening equipment. Today, the industry promoting health checks continues to promote (and profit from) these tests though, I am pleased to say that a growing number of doctors now share my fear that such tests may, in the long run, do far more harm than good.

Here's just one of many examples I can give.

In 1988, I first warned about the danger of mammograms in a (now out of print) book called *The Health Scandal*. My criticism was, of course, greeted with howls of outrage from the medical establishment. Back then I wrote: 'There are, of course, risks in having regular X–ray examinations. No one knows yet exactly what those risks are. We will probably find out in another ten or twenty years time.'

In fact, it was in 2006 that doctors finally issued a warning about mammograms, coming to precisely the conclusion I had warned about eighteen years earlier. Mammographic screening may help prevent breast cancer. But it may also cause breast cancer. Just how many women die because of the radiation they have received through mammography isn't known but it seems that the risks for younger women (women in their 30s for example) are higher than the risks for older women. (Radiation induced cancer typically takes up to 20 years to develop so for a woman in her 80's the risks of mammography are probably somewhere between slight and negligible.) Does mammography cause more cancers than it helps to prevent? Would other forms of screening be safer and therefore more effective? I don't know. This is a decision that every woman has to make for herself. I certainly don't believe that anyone knows the answers to those questions with any certainty either. Personally, if pushed for an answer, I would have to say that I believe (as I did in 1988) that mammography should be stopped until some proper long–term testing has been done. It won't be of course. The commercial and political reasons for continuing with mammography are far too powerful.

I have a personal reason for being wary of screening tests.

Twenty five years ago an insurance company arranged for me to have a medical examination. I was perfectly healthy at the time. The examination showed a minute amount of blood in my urine. A subsequent ultrasound scan showed a deformed kidney. Surgeons were summoned. I was prepared for an operation. And then it was discovered that there was nothing wrong with my kidneys. It was the tests, not me, that needed treatment.

My suspicion of screening tests pre–dates that experience. But the experience reinforced my fears and suspicions.

20. I have learned never to send anything by e–mail that I wouldn't be happy to see painted on a wall near my home.

If you want to say something private, say it in a letter, put the letter in an envelope, put a stamp on the envelope and post it. It may be a little slower, but it is still by far the most secure way to communicate.

Always use an e–mail address with your own name so that you will always remember that whatever you write isn't even private let alone secret.

21. I have learned not to trust either the BBC or the Internet as sources of impartial news and information.

In my view the main problem with the BBC is that it is biased. For example, the BBC tends to broadcast praise of the European Union but to suppress or ignore criticism of the organisation. It is absurd and unfair that British citizens should be forced to pay for the BBC's extravagances and prejudices by being compelled to pay an annual licence fee.

The Internet is useless as a source of information because so many of the sites which provide search facilities or news are biased in favour of advertisers. It is quite impossible to search the Internet and then trust the information or advice which you find unless you are expert enough in the field to be able to assess the value of the material you are reading. I find it alarming that many students (and not a few teachers) believe that the Internet has made textbooks irrelevant.

22. I have learned that Britain, America and Europe are going to remain in an economic mess for decades.

The huge debt created by the British Government's spend, spend, spend policies will mean that taxes will have to rise, and stay high, while Government spending will have to fall. There is no alternative scenario. The consequences will be disastrous. Unemployment will rise. Interest rates will rise. Inflation will soar. House prices will fall or remain stagnant.

And the nation's infrastructure will deteriorate.

Britain is awash with highly paid bureaucrats. And in times of economic crisis the one thing bureaucrats do not do is fire themselves or reduce the size of their administrative departments. And so, inevitably, the services the Government provides will deteriorate. Health care, education, roads – every service the Government spends our money on will show a significant fall in quality. The deterioration will be exacerbated by the fact that these services will have to be shared with a growing number of immigrants pouring in from the European Union (although as the services provided in the UK fall, so the number of immigrants wanting to come to Britain, and the number wanting to stay, will fall.)

23. I have learned that hospitals are not suitable places for sick people. If you must go into one, you should get out as quickly as you can.

Before the industrial age hospitals were built like cathedrals in order to lift the soul and ease the mind. Hospitals were decorated with carvings, works of art, flowers and perfumes. Modern hospitals are built with no regard for the spirit, eye or soul. They are bare, more like prisons than temples, designed to concentrate the mind on pain, fear and death. Where there are windows they are positioned in such a way that patients can't see out of them (though even if they could they probably wouldn't be able to see anything more enthralling than the refuse bins or the air conditioning units). If there are windows with good views then those windows will be on the sides of offices occupied by bureaucrats. The most highly paid bureaucrats get the best views.

But patients aren't just in danger because hospitals are badly designed and badly run.

One of the reasons why hospitals are no longer suitable for sick people is the fact that ambitious, modern nurses want to administer rather than nurse.

In the dark old days nurses were hired and trained to nurse. Aspiring nurses (mostly but not exclusively female) were inspired by the desire to tend and to heal. Nursing was a noble profession. Caring was the key word. The most powerful jobs in the profession were occupied by ward sisters and matrons – all of whom still had close, daily contact with patients.

Sadly, today's career structure means that nurses whose desire to nurse is accompanied by even the slightest ambition must quickly move up the ladder to a point where they spend very little time with patients. Many senior nurses now spend their days closeted in their offices, staring at computer screens and filling in assessment forms. Many seem to regard themselves as above what they see as the menial tasks of nursing. They leave the hands–on work to untrained staff. The introduction of degrees for nurses has made things even worse by turning a fundamentally practical profession into one with entirely spurious academic ambitions. The modern career structure for nurses has taken the best nurses away from patients. The drive for this career structure was driven by a patronising and entirely inaccurate concept: that nursing is demeaning.

Today, many nurses go into the profession attracted not by the desire to tend the sick but by the salaries, perks, authority and career structure which will, they know, take them away from practical work. The system is designed to attract exactly the wrong people into nursing.

The actual hands–on nursing is done, very largely, by junior staff.

This is, without a doubt, one of the reasons why modern hospitals are so bad and it is the reason why serious hospital infections are now endemic; it is why nurses are too often rude and uncaring to patients and why, in so many hospitals, clusters of nurses are more likely to be found having meetings (more appropriately called coffee–breaks) than actually helping patients. It is, for example, why thousands of elderly patients are left in pain, left to starve to death, left to die of dehydration, left in soiled bedclothes and left, ignored and without dignity, while nurses complete their paperwork.

Time and time again patients report that nurses won't lift them up the bed (it has been reported that some hospitals have posters with the slogan 'Nurses are not weightlifters' on their walls), won't help feed them, won't bring bedpans, won't change beds, won't do anything for patients in pain or distress and won't respond when the call button is pressed. They will not, in short, do any of the things that nurses are traditionally supposed to do. They are not interested in soothing or healing or helping because, even at quite junior levels, they have become career administrators with ambitions.

In many hospitals it is the patients who can get out of bed who end up doing all the nursing work.

Stop a nurse in a modern hospital and ask her where such and such a patient can be found, or how he or she is progressing, and you will probably be met with a glazed, disinterested look. They don't know and they don't much care. Private hospitals, where patients pay directly for their care, are a little better.

24. I have learned that the world isn't just running out of oil but is also running out of just about all natural resources.

For decades American Governments have identified sources of materials in Third World countries and have then encouraged American companies to remove those resources for American use. For years the Chinese and the Indians were content to enjoy their fairly simply lifestyles (by Western values) and to let the Americans steal everything of value.

No more.

Today, the people of China and India want what they call an American way of life. They want smart houses, two cars, two television sets, air conditioning, a dishwasher, a refrigerator and a deep freeze filled with harmburgers and ice cream. They want computers and computer games and all the rest of the American dream.

If the rate of growth which China has exhibited for the last few years continues, then the entire Chinese nation will soon be as rich as the Americans are today. Within a couple of decades everyone in China will have an American style house and a couple of cars.

They will want to eat meat and eggs instead of rice. They will want to eat more of everything. And they will want everything nicely packaged.

This is not a wild forecast.

This is not even a prediction.

It's happening.

In a few years time the Chinese will use up more oil than is currently being produced for worldwide consumption. They will consume as much grain as is being produced for worldwide consumption. They will use more steel than the whole of Europe and America. They will be responsible for more than doubling the number of cars on the planet. To satisfy their yearning for magazines, invoices and parking tickets the production of paper will have to double.

That's just China.

Within a few years India will have a bigger population than China. The Indian economy is growing almost as fast as the Chinese economy.

And then there's the rest of Asia. And Russia. And Eastern Europe. And Africa.

It isn't difficult to see why the world is running out of everything. You think of it – wood, steel, copper, water – the world is probably running out of it.

The prices of metals such as copper and lead have risen dramatically in recent years. And I believe they are likely to continue to rise – even when oil starts to become more expensive. The Chinese are not going to suddenly stop making motor cars or television sets. However, when the peak oil crisis really hits these prices may fall (because the demand for metals will drop).

We are using up the world's resources in general, and its minerals in particular, at an alarming rate.

If the world keeps going at its present rate then almost all minerals will run out in a decade or two's time.

Uranium and the base metals will, I believe, all continue to rise in price in the near and mid–term. In the long–term, however, I believe that only the precious metals with a currency link (gold and silver) will rise ever onwards and upwards.

There are many mining companies available for investment. The safest are probably the biggest. Huge multinational miners tend to have mines in different countries and they tend to produce and sell a variety of different metals. Smaller mines often specialise in finding particular metals and although their shares are invariably riskier the rewards can be much greater. A share in a small mining company may multiply tenfold or even more. On the other hand the company may disappear entirely and the shares become worthless.

Some small mining companies will have operating mines. Others will simply have licences to look for metals. In addition to the risk that a company may fail to find any metal there are political risks. A greedy government may confiscate land or take a large chunk of a successful mine. Some of the entrepreneurs who set up small exploration companies are roguish individuals who have spotted an opportunity and who are eager to make money out of gullible investors rather than out of digging metals out of the ground.

In the past, mining has been a cyclical business. The value of mining companies went up and down almost regularly. When the price of a commodity went down miners would close down mines and not open up new ones. The commodity would, therefore, become scarcer. When the metal became scarce enough the price would rise. And, in the nature of these things, the price would rise up to a level way beyond the level it had previously attained. At that point mining companies would start digging again. And entrepreneurs would raise capital to go exploring.

Soon there would be more than enough of the metal around. And the price would fall again.

This time things may be a little different.

(That is, I admit, the most dangerous thing anyone can believe about financial markets. It's what people say all the time. When dot.com shares went to ridiculous heights at the end of the 20th century all the enthusiastic analysts and investors were chanting 'this time it's different'. It wasn't of course. Prices collapsed and investors lost their shirts, trousers, shoes and socks.)

However, I believe things may be slightly different in mining because we're talking about commodities (metals) which are known to be available only in limited quantities. There is only so much copper available. Once it's gone you can't make any more. And if demand soars then the availability and price of the metal must alter. And although metals are running out, the demand for them is soaring. The industrial revolution boom has hit China, India and a dozen other rapidly growing countries all at the same time.

In mining, probably more than any other area of investment, geopolitical circumstances and the macroeconomic situation have always been crucial. And the geopolitical and macroeconomic circumstances mean that this time the upturn in the mining cycle is likely to be sharper and longer than usual.

There is, however, a big warning attached to mining companies: when the oil shortage becomes severe building programmes will have to stop. There won't be any oil for making cars so there won't be any need to build roads. New cities won't get built because the problems created by the oil shortage will be devastating.

At that point mining shares will crash.

There won't be much of a market for steel, copper or any other non–precious metals.

25. I have learned never to do private or confidential work on a computer which I use for Internet access.

I always store valuable information on portable disks, not on computer hard drives, and I always put copies in safe places.

26. I have learned that there are fashions in medicine just as much as there are fashions in clothes.

The difference is that whereas badly conceived fashions in clothes are only likely to embarrass you, ill–conceived fashions in medicine may kill you. The fashions in medicine have, by and large, as much scientific validity as the fashions in the rag trade.

The most obvious fashions in medicine relate to treatments. For example, a couple of centuries ago, enemas, purges and bleedings were all the rage. In 17th century France Louis XIII had 212 enemas, 215 purges and 47 bleedings in a single year. The Canon of Troyes is reputed to have had a total of 2,190 enemas in a two year period; how he found time to do anything else is difficult to imagine. By the mid 19th century enemas were a little last year's style and bleeding was the in–thing. Patients would totter into their doctor's surgery, sit down, tuck up their sleeves and ask the doctor to 'draw me a pint of blood'. Bleeding was the universal cure, recommended for most symptoms and ailments. Feeling a little under the weather? A little light bleeding should soon put you to rights. Constant headaches? We'll soon have that sorted for you, sir. Just roll up your sleeve. Bit of trouble down below, madam? Not to worry. Slip off your frock and hold your arm out.

A little later, in the 19th century, doctors put their lancets away and started recommending alcohol as the new panacea. Brandy was the favoured remedy in the doctor's pharmacopoeia. People took it for almost everything. And when patients developed delirium tremens the recommended treatment was more alcohol. If things got so bad that the brandy didn't work doctors added a little opium. Those were the days to be ill. Hypochondriacs must have had a wonderful time.

In the years from the 1930's onwards, removing tonsils became the fashionable treatment. Tonsils were removed from between a half and three–quarters of all children in the 1930's. This often useless and unnecessary (and always potentially hazardous) operation is less commonly performed these days but in the 1970's over a million such operations were done every year in Britain alone. Doctors used to rip out tonsils on the kitchen table and toss them to the dog. Between 200 and 300 deaths a year were caused by the operation. One suspects that few, if any, of those unfortunate children would have died from tonsillitis.

Diseases go in cycles too. In the early 19th century the fashionable diagnosis was 'inflammation'. Then, when patients and doctors tired of that, the new key word was 'debility'. Doctors didn't know terribly much and so their diagnoses, like their treatments, tended to be rather general.

These days patients expect more specific diagnoses and doctors are invariably happy to oblige.

One year everyone will be suffering from asthma. It will be the disease of the moment just as the mini skirt or ripped jeans may drift mysteriously in and out of fashion. Another year arthritis will be the fashionable disease as a drug company persuades journalists to write articles extolling the virtues (and disguising the vices) of its latest product. Depression. Irritable bowel syndrome. Osteoporosis. The cycle is a relatively simple one. The drug company with a new and profitable product to sell (usually designed for some long–term – and therefore immensely profitable – disorder) will send teams of well–trained representatives around to talk to family physicians, give them presents and take them out for expensive luncheons. The sales representatives will be equipped with information showing that the disorder in question is rapidly reaching epidemic proportions, lists of warning symptoms for the doctor to watch out for and information about the drug company's new solution to the problem. Because the product will be new to the market there will probably be very little evidence available about side effects and the sales representative will be accurately able to describe the drug as extremely 'safe'. There are even non–existent diseases (ADHD is perhaps the best known) which seem to me, and, I suspect, a growing number of other physicians, to have been originally invented in order to find a use for expensive medicinal compounds (and enthusiastically welcomed by parents who find the fictitious disease to be a handy and enormously useful explanation for bad behaviour).

Not surprisingly, thousands of family doctors will respond to this hard sell system by diagnosing more of the disease in question and handing out fistfuls of prescriptions for the recommended product. Older drugs, well–tried, possibly effective and probably safer than the new replacement, will be discarded as out–of–date. After all, their side effects will, over the years, have been well–documented.

As the disease subsequently seems to become more widespread so articles will appear about it in newspapers and magazines and television pundits will start to talk about it. Every patient who has the appropriate symptoms (however mildly) will be convinced that he or she is suffering from the disease in question.

And the number of prescriptions being written for the new wonder product will soon rocket – pushing up drug company profits dramatically.

Then, a year or so later, patients and doctors alike will become aware of the many side effects associated with the new alleged wonder product and prescribing levels will fall. It is then the turn of some other product and some other disease to take the limelight and some other drug company to enjoy a dramatic boost in its profits.

27. I have learned that debt can cause great pain.

The latter part of the 20th century was, without a doubt, the era of greed. Millions of people fought hard not to acquire a decent standard of living but to get everything. Humans went from needs to wants, through luxury to excess. Moral, ethical, environmental, cultural, emotional, spiritual and personal consequences were ignored in the search for more stuff.

Entrepreneurs who were enjoying their work made their businesses bigger. They borrowed money to expand. And then they found they needed accountants, lawyers and other specialists. The man who used to enjoy his work found that the more successful he became the less time he spent doing what he originally wanted to do with his life. He spent most of his time in meetings and preparing for meetings. What was left he spent talking to the banks about his debts.

Shopping became a hobby, a recreation ('retail therapy', 'shop till you drop') and, for many, an addiction. Work became a constant grind. Instead of going to work to 'earn a living' people were earning but no longer living. Work had become a source of money and there could never be enough (or too much) of that. Earning and spending, owing and worrying.

Money became an end rather than a means. Money was no longer a way to buy food and pay for shelter and nor was it something to use to purchase treats and delights. Acquiring money – and then spending it – had become everything. And we were encouraged in this belief by advertisers (who wanted our money themselves) and by politicians (who wanted us to keep spending so that the economy would grow and they could disguise the fact that the State itself had a huge spending problem). To them we are consumers and taxpayers. Nothing more. At times of national economic crisis people are actually encouraged to go out and shop for their country.

Millions learnt the superficial short–term joys of debt. People didn't just borrow money to buy a home (though they did that in huge quantities). They also borrowed money to buy cars (why share one when you can have one each – besides with two jobs, necessary to bring in the money to pay all the bills, two cars became essential), kitchen equipment, huge flat–screen digital televisions and computers. They borrowed money to make sure that everyone in the house had a telephone of their own. They borrowed money so that they could talk to their neighbours on the telephone (so much more satisfying than leaning on the garden fence, which can't be as much fun because it costs nothing). They borrowed money to go on holiday. They borrowed money to buy second homes. And, of course, they borrowed money to buy smart clothes to wear for work. They borrowed money to buy the season ticket for the train to get to work. They borrowed money to pay for expensive snacks bought to eat on the train or while rushing from one appointment to the next. They borrowed money to pay the interest on the money they had borrowed.

Most alarming of all is the fact that millions of people with horrifying debts now genuinely believe that their situation is not their fault. They prefer to blame the banks which lent them the money rather than to acknowledge their own greed. Most didn't seem to realise that debt creates shackles. To pay their debts (and the debts their debts themselves accrued) people are forced to continue with work they hate. They cannot afford to quit; to walk away and do something they might enjoy. They cannot even afford to pause, rethink and replan their lives. Every small threat becomes a major stress. A temporary illness, an inability to work, becomes a huge problem. The threat of unemployment is a nightmare when credit card bills are pouring through the letterbox.

Real dreams, hopes and aspirations are forgotten; pushed aside by plastic dreams, cardboard hopes and tinsel aspirations. The essentials in life are drowned by the non–essentials. In the same way that savings can provide freedom so debt will inevitably produce slavery.

People may appear affluent but their noses are stuck to the grindstone as they work ever harder to keep the banks and loan companies off their backs.

The problem with our recommended lifestyle is that when your life is designed to accumulate then what you have is never enough. More is always better and 'enough' is always a distant, unattainable horizon. If more is better then what we have can never be enough. There is always more 'more'.

No one ever slows down long enough to realise that if they don't have two jobs they won't need two cars. Born to work. Born to shop. Whoever dies with the most toys is the winner and gets the biggest obituary. (Though those with the most toys have, paradoxically, probably worked so hard to pay for them that they have played with them very little.) Life, liberty and the pursuit of a bigger television set.

Survey after survey show that the majority of people find their work boring and stressful. People complain that they have no free time and no time for hobbies. The divorce rate rises and rises (the vast majority of divorces being caused by arguments over money not sex). Anxiety and depression are often blamed on stress caused by worrying about work and money.

Work and money.

Our identities have become our work and our shopping; our earning and our spending. We are worth what we earn. A top television performer in the USA has a clause in his contract confirming that he will always be paid $1 more than the next highest paid performer at the network. Why? What does it matter to him what anyone else gets paid?

Our self–regard is tied up with the stuff we have bought with the money we've borrowed. Our status is determined not by what we have done or learnt or contributed, nor even by what we have acquired through our hard work, but by what we have acquired through borrowing. Our success is measured by our capacity to borrow.

We think we are working to pay the bills but we end up spending more than we earn on more than we need. And when our only joy is shopping we make things worse for ourselves. We shop to cheer ourselves up (a new outfit, a bottle of wine, a visit to the hairdresser, a trip to Disneyland). We buy books about hobbies rather than actually spending time doing them ourselves. We watch television programmes about other people experiencing life because we are too busy to do it ourselves.

Debt: the most destructive of addictions.

28. I have learned never to use my passport for anything except passing through customs.

Don't tell the bank you have one and you won't have to show it. Similarly, guard your National Insurance number as carefully as you can. Use a gas bill in preference to something more personal.

When forced to provide documentation to prove that you are who you say you are, provide the least important piece of paper you can find.

29. I have learned not to sign trivial forms with the same signature I use for legal documents or cheques.

I do not use accurate information for trivial enquiries where it is not legally required. If I am asked for my mother's maiden name on an Internet website I try to be imaginative (as long as what I am doing does not break the law).

The only problem lies in remembering whether my mother's maiden name is Crippen or Borgia.

30. I have learned to be a sceptical investor.

If it sounds too good to be true – then I don't buy it. If I don't understand it – then I don't buy it. If I don't understand how the seller can make money – then I don't buy it. If it sounds too good to be true then it probably isn't true – and I don't buy it.

31. I have learned to be a contrarian investor.

Experience tells me that I won't go far wrong if I buy what most people are selling and sell what most people are buying.

Successful investment is largely about courage. If you go with the crowd (buying what everyone else is buying) you will be no more of a success than everyone else. Because of costs, expenses, fees and taxes most investors (amateur and professional) do worse than the market.

But I have also learned that as a contrarian investor I must always make sure

I understand why other people think the way they do. And I always want to be sure that I can see the faults in their arguments. Listen to what other people are saying. But do so not because you want to follow their investment advice but because you want to know what they are saying (and probably doing).

If you want to beat the market you have to outthink the majority of other investors (both professionals and amateurs). That is as easy as it sounds. If you are daunted by that prospect you may succeed. If you are not daunted by the prospect you will probably not succeed.

If you're going to add value to your investments then someone else has to lose money. That's the way it works. Adding value to your investments is a zero–sum game. In order to add value you must know or understand things which most other investors do not know or understand or are not prepared to accept. And you must be able to think independently and think conceptually. You will also need the confidence to go against the crowd. Remember, that you will be competing with highly paid professionals who are equipped with hugely expensive resources.

32. I have learned to remember why I am investing.

The aim is to make money. Do not feel shy or embarrassed about this. If your aim is to make the world a better place, put your money to work in some more direct way. I will not invest in companies of whose activities I disapprove (pharmaceutical companies, arms companies and tobacco companies, for example). And I will invest in companies which may improve the world. But the bottom line is that if investments don't make money (either as dividends or capital gains) then they are failing.

33. I have learned that if I want to do well at something then I have to focus.

Top golfers don't try to win tennis championships. The more you focus the better you will do.

34. I have learned to develop my instincts and to learn to listen to them.

A decade or two ago you would have had difficulty in finding any reputable scientist prepared to admit that he believed in telepathy or extra sensory perception. These days you'd have as much difficulty in finding a reputable scientist prepared to say categorically that he did not believe in parapsychology.

As the whole subject becomes better known, so increasing numbers of people provide us with practical illustrations of the remarkable ways in which the mind often operates. There have been countless stories of individuals having dreams and then discovering that their dreams were very close to reality. The mind, it seems, can work in many remarkable ways.

One continuing problem is that it is only too easy to pick out specific instances and examples of intuition and to then exaggerate or distort their importance. But even allowing for this, there is little doubt that most of us do have skills that we use only too rarely. Nor is there any doubt that by taking greater advantage of these skills we could deal with many of our daily problems far more readily, and with far less stress and heartache.

If you tend to spend ages making relatively minor decisions – and find yourself getting into quite a state trying to decide what to wear, what to eat and so on – then give yourself a ten–second limit for making your decision. You'll find this a remarkably liberating exercise. Simply make up your mind to follow whatever thought sprang first into your mind. If your first instinct was to put on your red dress or blue suit, do just that. Don't waste mental energy thinking about it for an hour and trying on everything in your wardrobe. Similarly, if your first instinct tells you to order the mushrooms, order them. Don't spend half an hour worrying about whether to order the mushrooms or the melon. The chances are that your first, instinctive solution was probably the best. And with fairly minor decisions like these you haven't got much to lose anyway. The longer you spend worrying before coming to a conclusion, the greater the price you'll have to pay for defying your sense of intuition.

If you have a difficult problem to solve and you've spent hours worrying about it, give up and do something completely different. Take a walk or a warm, relaxing bath. Or sit down in front of the fire with an entertaining book. The chances are that the best solution will be quite clear to you after an interval of an hour or so. Your subconscious mind will have continued to work on the problem and will have produced a solution for you.

When you're looking for a solution to a major problem, try writing down a string of possible answers. Scribble them down just as fast as you possibly can. Do this for ten or fifteen minutes or so and then sit down and look at what you've produced. You'll find that many of the things you've written down look silly or downright stupid. These can be discarded straight away. But many of the others will be useful. One of your jottings will very probably be the solution you are looking for.

Learn to listen to your instincts. Don't always fight your feelings. If you always fight your instincts you will never be comfortable.

35. I have learned that just as there is never a good time for a light bulb to go 'phut' so now is always the most difficult time to make a decision.

36. I have learned not to waste my life sitting on committees or going to meetings.

I haven't been to a meeting, or sat on a committee, for nearly 40 years and my life has been the better for it.

Most people fill their lives with pointless social clutter. They go to meetings which make no difference to anything. They watch television programmes for no very good reason other than that they have been broadcast. They go to parties, dinners and power breakfasts because they have been asked or because other people expect them to attend. These things take so much time, so many hours that will never return, but offer so little real reward.

I have no doubt that I would have been far more commercially successful as a writer if I had spent more time attending meetings and sipping white wine with agents, publishers and journalists. But I very much doubt if I would have been happier.

37. I have learned that money provides freedom and independence.

Money can give you the opportunity to say 'No' when you want to say 'No'. Money can give you a voice.

38. I have learned that diversification is one of the basic watchwords for investment.

'Don't put all your eggs in one basket,' is a sensible piece of advice. But you can, as always, have too much of a good thing.

If you invest in everything available then dealing costs and management costs and taxes and so on will decimate your profits. And any profits you make from good investments will be lost among the losses you make from your not–such–good investments. The moral is a simple one: if you think you've found a good investment idea, put a decent sized chunk of your money into it so that, if you're proved right, the profits will make an appreciable difference to your life.

'As time goes on, I get more and more convinced that the right method in investment is to put fairly large sums into enterprises which one thinks one knows something about and in the management of which one thoroughly believes,' said John Maynard Keynes. 'It is a mistake to think that one limits one's risk by spreading too much between enterprises about which one knows little and has no reason for special confidence...One's knowledge and experience are definitely limited and there are seldom more than two or three enterprises at any given time in which I personally feel myself entitled to put full confidence.'

39. I have learned that we ask ourselves 'Why?' too infrequently. It's the best and simplest question in the world.

'It is not enough to be busy,' said Henry David Thoreau. 'The question is: what are you busy about?'

Why do you work so hard? Why are you trying to make money? Why do you buy the things you buy? Why do you do what you do? Why does any of it matter? Why do you seek power? Why do you want this or that experience?

Most people ask themselves 'Why?' far too infrequently.

We live in a workaholic culture where most of us take on far too many commitments — many of which have no real value — simply because we feel we should.

For example, many car owners wash their motor vehicles once a week. They devote several hours of a weekend morning to this task. I wonder how many of them ever ask themselves why they are doing this — and whether the price they are paying (in terms of time, effort and money) is worth the dividend.

I can think of several possible reasons (other than the fact that it is merely a long established habit).

a) Because if a car is washed regularly it will fetch a better price when it is sold

b) Because a clean and shiny car is more likely to impress people

c) Because it is fun

Now, if a man gets pleasure from washing his car then that is fine. It is rather sad but I wouldn't dream of discouraging him. In fact, I would be happy for him to pop round on Sunday morning and wash my car too if it would give him pleasure.

But, if he chooses either of the other two reasons then I would encourage him to think hard about the way he is spending his time.

Let's concentrate on answer a) to begin with: the hope that by washing his car regularly he will be able to get a better price for it when he comes to sell it.

If he washes the car once a week and spends three hours on the task that is approximately 150 hours a year. In three years (the average time for which a car is likely to be kept) that is 450 hours.

Now, work out how much more you think a regularly washed car is likely to fetch when it is sold and subtract the cost of washing and polishing materials. This is figure A.

Then take the total number of hours spent on cleaning the car in between purchasing it and selling it. This is figure B.

Finally, divide figure A by figure B to obtain the hourly rate you are effectively paying yourself for car cleaning.

You will, I suspect, be horrified to discover just how little it is.

Now, let's turn to answer b).

What is the point of spending hours every week washing a car simply so that people you don't know, and will probably never meet, will be impressed?

Is this really the best use of your time?

It is possible to apply this simple questioning to just about everything you do.

It is even possible to apply it to work itself.

Many men (and a growing number of women) do not seem to realise that they are caught on a treadmill which is taking them absolutely nowhere.

They could completely or partly retire and live very comfortably on what they have already made. But they don't.

If they were working because they enjoyed their work that would be understandable.

But how many men or women can honestly say that they thoroughly enjoy their work?

Many working men and women are pushing themselves for no reason; they are engaged in a race where the grave is the only goal and a headstone the only prize. They sacrifice their personal lives for work from which they obtain little or no satisfaction. The only goal is making money. The money is the prize, the glory, the passion and the purpose.

And the money making ritual continues because people don't ask themselves: 'Why?' and 'So what?'

Ask yourself 'Why?' you do everything you do.

Is it for applause and public approbation? Is it because you have an urgent need to say something? Is it because you want to make money for some specific purpose? Is it because you believe that you know what is right and what is wrong? Is it because you want to right a wrong? Is it because the incompetence and dishonesty of others has inspired you to action?

Not until you know why you do something will you be able to do it effectively. Why settle for less life and less control over your time than you could have? (And remember to ask yourself what happened to the dreams you had when you were 16–years–old.)

Remember that you are now enjoying tomorrow's good old days. You should do whatever you can to make each day the best day of your life. When you get to the end of your life you should be able to look back and say: 'I gave it my best shot!'

Make sure you are doing everything you can with your life. Ask yourself why you are doing something and you may find yourself surprised by the answer. Ask yourself 'Why?' and 'So what?' whenever you plan to do something.

The answers you get may change your life.

Why do you want a better job? Why do you want to save money? Why do you want to move house? Why do you want to buy a holiday home?

Only when you ask yourself 'Why?' will you know what you really need and what you are prepared to do for it.

Most people earn and spend without ever asking themselves 'Why?' They blindly sell their time (which is the same as selling their lives) for money which they spend on things they neither want nor need.

Ask yourself 'Why?' more often and you will learn more about yourself and what you are doing.

But be warned. Asking yourself this simple question can be unnerving. You may get answers.

And if you have been going through life for years without knowing where you were headed (or why) then you may find the answers you get rather startling.

40. I have learned to expect the unexpected.

However much you know, you will never know more than a tiny percentage of the relevant facts. The only constant in our lives is change. And the only thing that will always happen is the unexpected.

The things you are expecting hardly ever happen (and because you are expecting them they are probably already discounted). It is the things you aren't expecting which will change your life.

Always leave space in your life for the unexpected. If you fill your days then you will always be under intolerable stress because there will always be crises and you will always struggle to find time to deal with them.

It is the unexpected things that will affect your life most dramatically. The events you are expecting will probably have a relatively mild effect. Unexpected, small incidents can often produce a quite disproportionate response.

41. I have learned that anyone who works for the Government, the council or a company which has branches is one of 'them'. And should always be regarded as such.

42. I have learned not to expect the authorities to protect me.

They will not. I have learned not to expect compensation when I have been deceived. And I have learned not to waste too much of my life complaining through official complaints procedures.

Official complaints systems are designed to protect officials from complainants. Accountability is no longer a recognised concept among those employed by the State to provide services for the general public.

Don't use their complaints systems. Their complaints systems exist to protect them. In the NHS, for example, the complaints processes seem to me designed to protect NHS employees, rather than to protect the interests of patients. And within any large organisation the complaints system is 'theirs'. The employees know how the system works; they understand it; they know how to use it and they do not fear it. I honestly don't think it is worthwhile bothering to complain if you are going to use the official system. If you complain 'their' way then you will probably end up with your original unhappiness compounded by frustration and a sense of great injustice.

It is much better to use outside complaints procedures. Make a complaint to the press. Or use the Human Rights Act. It is very easy for bureaucrats and administrators to fall foul of the Human Rights Act and it is my experience that most public employees are terrified of the Act.

If you use your imagination when complaining you may find that even the most aggressive, unpleasant tyrant will become vulnerable.

43. Learn, and be aware of, the Human Rights Act.

Although it is frequently abused (usually by lawyers representing thieves, murderers and objectionable ne'er do wells from many sources) this is the only recently enacted piece of legislation which serves to protect the individual against the State.

The Human Rights Act has been used by terrorists, criminals, and illegal asylum seekers and a whole host of others. It has been used by gypsies and travellers to enable them to breach planning laws.

It is, so we are told, the Human Rights Act which is responsible for much of the politically–correct nonsense which now besieges our society. It is the Human Rights Act which explains much of the blatant injustice in our society.

There is little doubt that there are few things which have damaged the very fabric of English society more than the Human Rights Act.

But everyone – even white, middle class English folk – can use the Human Rights Act. That is the whole point of it.

I have printed below a summary of the articles of the Human Rights Act. It shouldn't take you too long to see how you too can take advantage of this probably well–meaning but impractical legislation. The best advertisement for its usefulness is the fact that you only have to mention the words 'human', 'rights', 'act', in succession to see bureaucrats and civil servants wilt and cabinet ministers shiver and pale.

At the end of the list of 'Articles' I have added a list of protocols (later additions to the Convention). If you read through these carefully I feel sure that you may find ways to take advantage of some of these 'rights' too. (Ironically, I consider that much of the EU's own legislation is in breach of the Human Rights legislation.)

Article 1: (is the introduction to the Act).

Article 2: Right to Life.

You have the absolute right to have your life protected by law. There are only certain very limited circumstances where it is acceptable for the State to take away someone's life, e.g. if a police officer acts justifiably in self–defence.

Article 3: Prohibition of Torture

You have the absolute right not to be tortured or subjected to treatment or punishment which is inhuman or degrading.

Article 4: Prohibition of Slavery and Forced Labour

You have the absolute right not to be treated as a slave or forced to perform certain kinds of labour.

Article 5: Right To Liberty And Security

You have the right not to be deprived of your liberty – 'arrested or detained' – except in limited cases specified in the Article (e.g. where you are suspected or convicted of committing a crime) and where this is justified by a clear legal procedure.

Article 6: Right To A Fair Trial

You have the right to a fair and public hearing within a reasonable period of time. This applies to both criminal charges against you, or in sorting out cases concerning your civil rights and obligations. Hearings must be by an independent and impartial tribunal established by law. It is possible to exclude the public from the hearing (though not the judgement) if that is necessary to protect things like national security or public order. If it is a criminal charge you are presumed innocent until proved guilty according to law and have certain guaranteed rights to defend yourself.

Article 7: No Punishment Without Law

You normally have the right not to be found guilty of an offence arising out of actions which at the time you committed them were not criminal. You are also protected against later increases in the possible sentence for an offence.

Article 8: Right To Respect For Private And Family Life

You have the right to respect for your private and family life, your home and your correspondence. This right can only be restricted in specified circumstances (such as protecting the public health or safety, preventing crime and protecting the rights of others.)

Article 9: Freedom of Thought, Conscience and Religion

You are free to hold a broad range of views, beliefs and thoughts, as well as religious faith. Limitations are permitted only in specified circumstances (such as protecting the public health or safety, preventing crime and protecting the rights of others).

Article 10: Freedom of Expression

You have the right to hold opinions and express your views on your own or in a group. This applies even if they are unpopular or disturbing. This right can only be restricted in specified circumstances (such as protecting the public health or safety, preventing crime and protecting the rights of others).

Article 11: Freedom of Assembly and Association

You have the right to assemble with other people in a peaceful way. You also have the right to associate with people, which can include the right to form a trade union. These rights can only be restricted in specified circumstances (such as protecting the public health or safety, preventing crime and protecting the rights of others).

Article 12: Right To Marry

Men and women have the right to marry and start a family. The national law will still govern how and at what age this can take place.

Article 13: There is no article 13.

Article 14: Prohibition of Discrimination

In the application of the Convention rights, you have the right not to be treated differently because of your race, religion, sex, political views or any other status, unless this can be justified objectively. Everyone must have equal access to Convention rights, whatever their status.

Article 1 of Protocol 1: Protection of Property

You have the right to the peaceful enjoyment of your possessions. Public authorities cannot usually interfere with things you own or the way you use them except in specified limited circumstances.

Article 2 of Protocol 1: Right To Education

You have the right not to be denied access to the educational system.

Article 3 of Protocol 1: Right To Free Elections

Elections for members of the legislative body (e.g. Parliament) must be free and fair and take place by secret ballot. Some qualifications may be imposed on those that are eligible to vote (e.g. a minimum age).

Articles 1 and 2 of Protocol 6: Abolition of the Death Penalty

These provisions abolish the death penalty. There can be limited exceptions in times of war but only in accordance with clearly specified laws.

The Human Rights Act must be obeyed by all public authorities (Government Ministers, civil servants, your local authority, your health authority and agencies such as the police, the courts and private companies when carrying out public functions). All new laws must fit in with your rights under the Human Rights Act. (Worryingly, the police and the politicians don't always seem to understand their legal obligations. Human rights judges have called for an end to the policy of the police holding onto DNA samples from citizens arrested but never convicted of any offence. The judges said that storing such information breached privacy rights. The police have, however, been allowed by the Government to continue collecting and storing DNA samples and to resist requests to have them deleted.)

One of the specific rights given by the Human Rights Act is the fundamental right to assembly – a right to meet with others for whatever reason you like (as long as it is lawful). If the police or public authorities are thinking of banning a demonstration or restricting marches they cannot impose a blanket ban. They cannot go further than is necessary to guard against the expected risks to others.

44. I have learned that it is not wise to entrust money to companies which are dependent upon the British Government for survival.

It is my belief that in future companies which are dependent upon the Government will not do well. Financial commentators claim that in a recession it is safe to invest money in companies which rely on Government patronage. In theory this makes sense. In a well–run country the Government would endeavour to limit the depth of the recession by spending money on building roads, schools and hospitals. But Britain is not (and has not been) a well–run country. The country is darned near bankrupt. The Government may want to spend loads of money on repairing old bits of infrastructure, and building new bits. But it simply doesn't have the money to do this. The next decade is, I fear, going to be fairly gloomy (and steadily become gloomier) for companies which rely entirely on Government patronage.

45. I have learned that doctors and nurses know surprisingly little about staying healthy.

Doctors have never taken much interest in preventive medicine. This, I'm afraid, is because they have little (or, rather, no) financial interest in keeping their patients healthy. Except in China (where doctors were once paid only for as long as their patients stayed well) doctors have always earned their money out of diagnosing and curing illness. When you earn money out of making people healthy when they are ill, keeping them healthy makes no financial sense at all.

46. I have learned to back my own judgement.

No one knows better than you do what is happening to the economy or the nation or the world. Mix a little common sense (that rarest of all commodities) in with your judgement and the chances are that your guesses will be better educated, and more accurate, than anyone else's.

There is no one more interested in your financial security than you.

It is not difficult to take control of your own financial future. And when you do make losses, make sure they are light and make sure you learn from them. Cut your losses and let your profits run. If you aren't prepared to take small losses you will probably have to accept big losses.

And, remember, you can gain even when you lose. If an investment goes wrong and you lose money, study what happened. Did you do something wrong? Were you just unlucky? Be brutally honest with yourself and you will learn from your losses.

47. I have learned that the Great British Pound (aka sterling) will remain in decline for some time.

Britain is the world's weakest western economy. (Technically, America is probably more bankrupt than Britain. But America has the world's reserve currency and Britain has a currency which will increasingly be seen as something of an embarrassment.)

For this reason I believe it is wise for me to buy shares in large, international companies which make most of their money outside the UK and make most of their money in a currency other than sterling.

48. I have learned that Britain's huge debts mean that interest rates are quite likely to soar in coming years.

The consequences will be devastating for many. Even those holding Government gilts will suffer because as interest rates rise so the value of gilts will fall. Pension fund companies which have stocked up on Government gilts, thinking them to be the safest form of investment, will be devastated.

Index–linked gilts (which provide some protection against inflation) are the ones I'm buying.

49. I have learned that governments print lots of new currency notes because it is an easy way to improve their exports.

This was a trick started in earnest by the Americans in the 1990's. It works because when you print more currency you lower the value of the stuff already in existence. And when the value of your currency falls when compared with the currencies of other countries your exports become cheaper.

All the world's major powers are now increasing their money supply. The Americans are increasing theirs massively. It is hardly surprising that the American dollar has been on a downward slide for years. This is not an accident. It is the American Government's deliberate policy. The dollar has lost more than seven eighths of its purchasing power over the last 60 years.

Of course, it isn't only the American dollar which has been destroyed by governments deliberately printing more money. The British Government has for years been printing huge amounts of new money. The European Bank has done the same. The British Pound, the Euro and even the once powerful Swiss Franc have all lost value in recent years. When I wrote this there was $40 trillion worth of paper money in the world and $50 trillion worth of bonds. A trillion is a million million or a thousand billion. I have no doubt that by the time you read this the numbers will be much, much higher.

Printing more money causes inflation, a liquidity bubble and absurd overvaluations in almost every market – from paintings to shares to houses.

50. I have learned to always use a Post Office box as a mailing address.

This reduces the number of people who have access to my home address. If anyone questions this (and they sometimes do) I point out that banks and HM Revenue and Customs will accept a PO Box address. And I point out that many official bodies and large companies themselves use a PO Box address. A very snotty banker once told me that only disreputable people used PO Boxes. I said I would write to his Head Office to complain about his remark. I asked him for the address. With his voice rich with embarrassment he then gave me a PO Box address (as I knew he would).

51. I have learned that the sector in which I choose to invest is more important than the share I choose to buy.

If retail shares do well then most retail shares usually go up. If banks do badly then most banking shares tend to fall together. If I believe that investing in oil will give me good profits then I invest in several large oil companies and several small ones.

Many investors spend a lot of their time trying to time the market or trying to pick stocks. A study in 1986 by Gary Brinson and colleagues called *The Determinants of Portfolio Performance* involved an analysis of 91 pension funds. The aim was to find out what decided performance most: asset allocation, stock–picking, market timing or costs.

The results showed that asset allocation (between stocks, bonds and cash) decided 94% of performance. Stock picking and market timing had no useful effect. The busiest fund managers seemed to harm their results by too much action (partly because trading involves costs).

The skill, it seems, lies not in choosing particular companies or properties to invest in, but in picking asset classes and investment cycles. If you invest at a time when the stock market is going up then it doesn't terribly much matter which shares you pick – most of them will go up. But if you invest at a time when the market is going down then most of the shares you choose will fall.

52. I have learned not to believe anyone who tells me that stock markets are efficient or logical.

They are neither. There was never much logic to the financial markets. Today, there is none whatsoever. Markets have always been influenced by two emotions: fear and greed. This has never been the case more than it is now. Stock markets are always assumed to be efficient. And they are also assumed to be ahead of the game. But they are neither. Stock markets are ruled by emotions.

53. I have learned that governments lie about inflation.

Governments tell two lies about inflation. First, they claim that inflation is a rise in prices which is outside their control and which they are struggling to hold back. This is the first lie. Inflation is caused by governments printing more money, and devaluing the stuff that is already in existence. If the government doubles the amount of currency in circulation then it halves the value of the money that's already out there. And it is that which then pushes up prices. So governments cause inflation. The second lie is the size of the problem. Inflation is much higher than they say it is.

The official figures exclude luxuries such as housing, energy and food. Education, pensions and healthcare are also routinely omitted – even though these are, for many people, the biggest costs in their budget. It is for this reason that people whose income is inflation–linked (people with inflation–linked pensions for example) find life difficult. And people whose incomes rise according to the official inflation figures also suffer. In order to retain your spending power (and your quality of life) you need to make much more than official inflation levels from your investments – otherwise your capital is shrinking. So if you don't take risks you are going to become poorer.

When the official level of inflation is 5% the real level of inflation will be at least double that. This means that if you are earning less than 10% a year on your investments you are losing money. With a lower official level of 2.5%, and an unofficial level of 5%, any increase in your capital of less than 5% means that you are losing money.

All this means that unless you are very rich, or are prepared to accept a deteriorating standard of living, you have to take some chances with your capital. Government policy means that you really don't have much choice.

Here are some things you should know about inflation:

1. Inflation was kept down at the end of the 20th century because we were importing cheap stuff from China. Cheap television sets, cheap bras and cheap shoes. This helped enormously in the 1980's and 1990's. It meant that we could buy more stuff with the money we had in our pockets and our bank accounts. But now the Chinese workers want higher wages. They want motor cars and they want television sets of their own.

2. The rate of inflation has a vital influence on the economy. Rising inflation means that interest rates have to go up. Rising inflation also means that monetary policy must be tightened. Falling inflation, on the other hand, results in lower interest rates and a booming economy. If inflation is not considered a threat, central bankers can reduce interest rates in order to stimulate a stagnant economy. But if inflation *is* considered a threat, central bankers will usually keep interest rates fairly high because they will worry that lower interest rates will over–stimulate the economy and produce more inflation. (Governments constantly claim to have found the way to conquer the 'boom and bust' economy. They are lying, of course.) The bull

market of the late 1980's and 1990's followed the high inflation rates and big bear of the 1970's. Falling inflation rates helped drive the powerful bull markets of the 1980's and 1990's. As inflation fell and productivity went up (as a result of new technology and as China and India started manufacturing things) so we did better and better. Cheapish oil made everything very easy. Those were the days when investors got, and learned to expect as normal, returns of 15% a year on their equity investments. If you wanted your money to grow there was no other game in town. Just buy shares and sit back and wait. And you didn't have to wait long.

3. In the middle of the 20th century, governments undermined the value of our money (and discouraged savings) by printing too many banknotes. The more money in circulation, the less the money is worth. Today, the amount of money in circulation (in the form of real notes) is only a tiny amount of the money available. Banks are now creating money by lending it as a debt (with interest attached, of course) and it is that practice which has really pushed up inflation. The whole problem started when bankers and politicians got rid of gold as a basis for our currencies. When governments could only print as much currency as they had gold the politicians were restrained. When the link with gold was abolished governments were free to print as much money as they wanted. Then they made things even worse by using computers to create seemingly endless supplies of 'imaginary' money. I recently bought a birthday card for my wife which cost more than I paid for my first car forty years ago. That's inflation. Inflation really does eat away at savings. If you had put £1,000,000 in a box under your bed 40 years ago it would now have a purchasing power of £77,000.

4. Paradoxically, politicians and central bankers love some inflation. The reason is simple. When the value of money goes down a little bit (which is what happens in inflation – you can buy less for your unit of currency) debts get washed away. If you are a government with huge debts then inflation is a wonderful thing. It helps diminish the value of your debts as time goes by. (By the same principle, inflation helps reduce the value of debt for everyone else, too.)

5. Rising commodity prices usually result in a rise in inflation in countries which have to import commodities. Countries which produce the commodities which are rising in value usually do well. I am very long–term bullish about the price of oil and other commodities (commodities of all sorts are running out and the demand for them is rising inexorably). I therefore believe that high inflation is likely to be a consistent problem in countries such as Britain (which rely on importing commodities such as oil). I also believe that countries such as Canada and Australia (which produce huge quantities of essential commodities) are likely to have a relatively strong future.

6. People think they are better off than they were twenty years ago because they earn more money. But, in reality, most are not better off because they can buy less with their money today than they were able to buy decades ago. When inflation soars it enables workers to have pay rises without the pay rises actually costing anything. But people aren't really better off.

7. Falsifying the inflation figures means that inflation proofed salaries and pensions paid by the Government can be increased by a much smaller figure than would be necessary if they were being increased by the real level of inflation.

8. Officially, inflation in the UK for the last 30 years has averaged 5.3% a year. That means that if you had money invested for that period and your after tax income was less than 5.3%, you were losing money. If you are a 40% taxpayer it's quite difficult to get an after tax income of 5.3% without taking considerable risks.

9. Governments use astonishing little tricks such as including hedonic adjustments and rental–equivalent home pricing and using geometric averaging when working out inflation figures. Geometric averaging means that if the basket of goodies measured to find the inflation figure contains one item which goes up 10% and another which goes down 10% the effect on the basket isn't 0% (as you might imagine) but a 1% fall. Governments produce this miracle of accounting by multiplying 110 (the figure obtained because of the 10% rise) by 90 (the figure obtained because of the 10% fall). This gives a total of 99. And, lo, a fall in inflation (and the cost of living) of 1%. Only politicians and economists can do this. Hedonic adjustments enable politicians to take advantage of progress to keep inflation low. If you bought a computer a year ago for £1,000 and you replace it with a computer which cost £1,500 but is 10 times as fast, then the computer is registered by the Government as costing less, even though in reality it cost more. And rental–equivalent home pricing? That's a trick they use to minimise the effect of rising house prices. If your home is now worth twice as much as it was a few years ago but the rent you would have to pay has only gone up by half then the inflation figure is deemed to be a half. The real rise in the cost of the home is ignored. All these utterly, deplorably dishonest inventions were designed to enable politicians to lie and cheat the voters. There are more tricks, (for example when they measure gross domestic product they tend to ignore the fact that the population has grown and that the per capita GDP – the figure that really matters – is probably going in the other direction) but I'm getting weary and I suspect you are too. Unravelling the lies they tell can be tiresome work. The people we hire to work for us have, as one, become the 'them' we have always feared.

10. Inflation is an invisible tax. Although it is a boon for borrowers (the £250,000 borrowed to buy a house shrinks as a result of inflation) it is a

curse for savers (the £250,000 pension fund shrinks in value and purchasing power as a result of inflation). Pensioners and others on a fixed income lose out because their buying power is constantly being eroded. Earners whose income rise doesn't match inflation (the real figure, rather than the false 'official' figure) also lose out. They may seem to be getting richer, as their income grows, but in reality they will be getting poorer. And everyone who pays tax will lose out. Tax thresholds do not usually rise with inflation. So, for example, stamp duty on house purchases affects an increasing number of people as house prices rise and the stamp duty thresholds remain the same. And since the point at which taxpayers find themselves liable for higher rates of tax tends to stay the same (or to rise nowhere near as much as inflation) the number of people paying higher tax rates is rising rapidly.

54. I have learned that there is no such thing as a safe investment.

If anyone tells you that an investment is 'safe' they are lying. Many so–called safe investments turn out to be the very opposite of safe. People who put their pension savings into Equitable Life pension funds found that 'safe' doesn't always mean quite what they thought it meant. Similarly, investors who bought Zero Dividend Preference Shares or Building Society Permanent Interest Bearing Shares found that 'safe' can sometimes be a shortened version of 'a good way to lose your money'.

And keeping your money in cash won't protect you. I believe that inflation is, in the future, likely to reach high levels. If inflation hits 20% then you will need to receive interest payments of 20% for your money just to keep pace with inflation.

Property is often regarded as a 'safe' investment. But I believe that property prices will fall dramatically. When petrol hits £50 a gallon (on its way ever upwards) and a loaf of bread costs £5 most people will be more concerned with staying alive than in investing in a larger house, a holiday home or a buy–to–let property.

I believe that many shares will prove to be unsafe too. Retailers (including supermarkets) will be hard hit when the oil price rises. Many transport companies, airlines, travel companies, computer companies, electrical goods suppliers and builders will disappear. So will mobile telephone companies and many banks. Any large company which depends on importing or exporting its products will be at risk. Estate agents are doomed as are most building companies and property companies. Clothing and shoe companies which rely on imports will be hard hit as will cosmetic companies and jewellers. Chemical companies will be in dire trouble.

Bonds will be dangerous too. If interest rates rise then bond prices will fall (since the yield must rise to keep the bonds attractive to investors).

55. I have learned to keep a healthy wodge of cash available.

Who knows when the roof is going to start leaking, the car is going to fall apart or the taxman is going to send an unexpected demand for money? Who knows when the banks will shut for a month or when the Government will restrict the amount of money you are allowed to take out of your account. (If you don't think that these things could happen then you haven't been paying attention.) If you have some cash you can deal with these problems. If you don't have any cash available you may have to sell investments at a terrible time.

56. I have learned that above average investment returns are usually a reward for taking risks.

Investors who do particularly well are usually taking big risks. They may do well for several years. But then they may have a bad year. In the long run they will be successful investors only if their good years far outweigh their bad years.

57. I have learned that investments should be for the long–term.

Unless there has been a major event causing you to rethink the reason for buying and continuing to hold you should not change your portfolio too often. Prices of shares and other investments move on a daily basis. But these movements are often irrelevant. However, it is important to understand that things move faster than they used to and although 'buy and hold' used to be a wise philosophy it is an approach which needs to be tempered. Consumer tastes, markets, geopolitical forces and technologies change – all these things mean that buying and holding any investment can be dangerous. But none of that alters the fact that if you buy and sell too frequently your profits will be decimated by dealing costs and by taxes.

58. I have learned that everything is going to get worse and nothing is going to be as good as it is today.

These, believe it not, are tomorrow's good old days.

59. I have learned that unhappy memories can often cause much mental (and even physical) pain.

But you can use the power of your imagination to help you get rid of unhappy memories from the past.

Here is what you do: think of the most embarrassing experience of your life; something that still haunts you. Try to get a clear picture of the incident in your mind. And then restructure the memory the way you would like it to have happened – and the way you would like to remember it.

For example, if you remember being asked to speak in public and making a complete fool of yourself simply rearrange your memory! Try to remember as much as you can about the incident. Remember the room in which it took place. Remember the weather outside. And the people who were present. And, then, instead of 'seeing' yourself looking a fool try to 'see' yourself speaking fluently and impressively and being rewarded with an ovation. Rerun your 'new' version of that once embarrassing memory once or twice every day for a week. After seven days the 'new' version will have started to replace the old, original, embarrassing version in your head. You will have rewritten history and started to erase an unhappy memory from your mind.

You can do this as often as you like – and get rid of all your old, embarrassing memories.

60. I have learned not to expect justice from the judiciary.

Those who expect justice are frequently disappointed. Justice and the law are widely separated.

61. I have learned that businesses are becoming outdated faster than ever.

There is, for example, no future in the airline industry or the newspaper industry. If you are contemplating starting a business, joining one or investing in one then you should try to understand how well that business will thrive during the coming years.

62. I have learned how to cut my cancer risk by 80%.

Doctors don't spend much time telling their patients how to avoid cancer – but they do spend enormous amounts of time, energy and money on treating cancer.

Astonishingly, doctors now know what causes 80% of all cancers. It is my view that you should be able to reduce your cancer risk by 80% by avoiding those 'triggers' which are known to be responsible for causing cancer.

Here is my advice:
1. Don't smoke tobacco and keep away from other people who smoke tobacco.
2. Cut your consumption of fatty food.

3.   Do not eat meat.
4.   Eat plenty of well–washed fresh fruit and vegetables.
5.   Eat plenty of fibre and whole grain foods.
6.   Do not have any unnecessary X–rays.
7.   Do not spend long periods of time in the sun.
8.   Try not to live underneath or close to electricity power lines or close to an electricity supply station. Do not sleep or sit too close to electrical appliances.
9.   Avoid foods which contain large quantities of additives.
10. Keep your weight under control.
11. Minimise your consumption of alcohol.
12. Avoid smoked, salt cured, salt pickled or barbecued foods.

63. I have learned that governments and bureaucrats aren't interested in facts or common sense.

Their policies are largely devised by, and for the benefit of, lobbyists and vested interests.

64. I have learned that most people take too many antibiotics and that doctors prescribe them recklessly.

When antibiotics – drugs such as penicillin – were first introduced in the 1930's they gave doctors a chance to kill the bacteria causing infections and to save the lives of patients who would otherwise have died of infections such as pneumonia. Antibiotics were regarded as genuine life–savers; heralding a revolution in health care.

Although it is certainly true that the impact made by antibiotics has been exaggerated (many of the diseases which are caused by organisms which are susceptible to antibiotics were on the decline before the antibiotics were introduced) these drugs are undoubtedly of considerable value.

The problem is that although doctors are aware of the advantages of these drugs (if they are in any doubt the drug companies will frequently remind them) they seem unaware of the hazards associated with their unnecessary use.

If you have a serious or troublesome infection – bronchitis, sore throat or cystitis for example – the chances are high that your doctor will prescribe an antibiotic.

If you are innocent and naive you might imagine that the prescribing of an antibiotic will have been done scientifically and that your doctor, as a man or woman of science, will have carefully chosen a drug specifically designed to eradicate the type of bug causing your infection and prescribed for precisely the right number of days.

You would, however, be quite wrong to assume that doctors know what they are doing when they prescribe antibiotics. Antibiotics are powerful drugs.

They do save lives. But, in general, they are prescribed with neither sound logic nor scientific understanding. The prescribing of antibiotics is a virtually random exercise. The average tapioca–brained traffic warden could prescribe them with as much sense and understanding as the average doctor. Visit one doctor with cystitis and she will give you enough antibiotics to last you for five days. Visit the doctor next door, complaining of exactly the same symptoms, and he may prescribe the same antibiotic but give you enough pills to last for seven days. And visit a third doctor and she may give you pills to last for ten or even fourteen days. Where, in the name of Areolus Phillipus Theophrastus Bombastus von Hohenheim, is the sense in any of this?

This bizarre situation occurs not because doctors haven't bothered to learn how to prescribe antibiotics but because no one knows how antibiotics should be prescribed. Astonishingly, no tests have ever been done to find out for precisely how long antibiotics should be given. Research scientists have been far too busy enjoying themselves doing unspeakable things to monkeys, cats and puppies to bother doing such useful or practical research.

All that is bad enough. But it isn't the end of the horror story. For although scientists know which antibiotics should be used to combat which bugs the evidence shows that the selection of a drug to prescribe is generally done with the sort of scientific judgement the average six–year–old might apply when picking a coloured sweet out of a box.

As any regular surgery goer will know, there are scores of antibiotics available. Some of these pills are simply variations on profitable themes. But there are some important differences between many of these pills. Drugs are designed to combat specific types of infection. However, most doctors don't usually bother to try to match antibiotics with bugs; instead they simply write out a prescription for any old drug. They tend to choose a drug because they like the name – or can spell it – rather than because it is appropriate.

The end result is that although you might think that the antibiotic you are prescribed has been chosen specifically for your infection you would probably be wrong. Your doctor will have probably simply picked a name at random. She is more likely to prescribe a drug because its name appears on the free disposable pen she happens to be holding than because she knows that it is the best and most suitable drug to kill the bug with which you are infected. Worse still, most doctors are so darned potty that they happily prescribe antibiotics for virus infections even though viruses are not susceptible to antibiotic therapy.

Today, one in six of the prescriptions doctors write is for an antibiotic and there are at least 100 preparations available for doctors to choose from. Sadly, there is no doubt that most of the prescriptions which are written for antibiotics are unnecessary. Many patients are suffering from viral infections which are not susceptible to antibiotics, and others would get better by themselves without any drug being prescribed. Various independent experts who have studied the use of antibiotics claim that between 50 – 90% of the prescriptions written for antibiotics are unnecessary.

To a certain extent doctors over–prescribe because they like to do something when faced with a patient – and prescribing a drug is virtually the only thing most of them can do. To some extent prescribing a drug is a defence against any possible future charge of negligence (on the basis that if the patient dies it is better to have done something than to have done nothing).

But the main reason for the over–prescribing of antibiotics is, without doubt, the fact that too many doctors are under the influence of the drug companies.

The over–prescribing of antibiotics would not matter too much if these drugs were harmless, and if there were no other hazards associated with their use. But antibiotics are certainly not harmless. I believe that antibiotics kill thousands of patients a year and if up to nine out of ten prescriptions for antibiotics are unnecessary then it is not unreasonable to assume that up to nine out of ten of those deaths are unnecessary too.

And antibiotics don't only kill patients. The unnecessary and excessive use of antibiotics causes allergy reactions, side effects and a huge variety of serious complications.

There is also the very real hazard that by overusing antibiotics doctors are enabling bacteria to develop immunity to these potentially life–saving drugs. There is now no doubt that many of our most useful drugs have been devalued by overuse and are no longer effective.

If your doctor prescribes an antibiotic for you don't be afraid to ask him whether you really need it. He may simply be prescribing the antibiotic because he thinks you will be disappointed if you don't get one.

The over–prescribing of antibiotics is not a new phenomenon.

In 1975, in my first book, *The Medicine Men*, I pointed out that one huge survey had shown that only one third of the patients given antibiotics had infections at all. Other surveys, I explained, had shown that even when patients do have an infection the antibiotic prescribed is usually the wrong one.

Nothing has improved since then. Today's doctors are just as criminally inept as their predecessors were. And members of the medical profession still treat me like a pariah for daring to expose these professional shortcomings.

But it is now clear that the warning about antibiotics which I gave decades ago was absolutely accurate. The careless, inaccurate and inappropriate prescribing of antibiotics by thousands of ignorant and careless doctors is one of the main reasons why a growing number of bugs are resistant to antibiotic therapy. Many once powerful drugs no longer work because doctors have handed them out like sweeties and bugs have been given the chance to grow stronger and more resistant to treatment. An ever–increasing number of patients are dying because antibiotics no longer work as well as they used to work.

During the last twenty five years I have made scores of predictions about health matters. Most of those predictions were laughed at by the medical establishment when I first made them. Nearly all of them have already come true.

I now add another prediction: infectious diseases will soon become one of the most feared and important causes of death – just as they were before the development of antibiotics. This tragic state of affairs will be the fault of those doctors who have overprescribed these drugs.

65. I have learned not to entrust anything I value to the Royal Mail.

I certainly don't use the ordinary post for truly sensitive or valuable documents. And I don't rely on the recorded delivery service. (The special delivery service is, I believe, the only reasonably acceptable way to send valuable documents through the post.) There are, it seems, an increasing number of crooks delivering or working with mail. Some of them probably got their jobs simply so that they could steal valuable items.

If you think I'm being unfair you should know that not even the Government trusts the Royal Mail with sensitive documents.

For example, the Passport Office doesn't use the Royal Mail to send out passports but chooses to use a courier. On the back of the envelope in which passports travel are the words: 'If delivered incorrectly please call (freephone number). Do not post in the Royal Mail.' These instructions are printed in red, capital letters.

And the Driver and Vehicle Licensing Agency tells drivers not to send debit card details through the post.

If I have something important to post I use a private carrier or courier and pay extra for insurance. If I do use the Royal Mail to deliver something important I use the special delivery service.

66. I have learned that repeat prescriptions are dangerous, and a major cause of serious illness.

A growing number of prescriptions (over half of all those written) are provided without there being any meeting between the doctor and the patient. The patient writes or telephones for a new supply of a specific drug and then, a day or so later, either collects or receives through the post the appropriate prescription.

This system of providing prescriptions 'on request' was originally designed to help patients suffering from chronic disorders such as diabetes, high blood pressure or epilepsy. Patients suffering from disorders which tend to vary very little over the months do not need daily, weekly or even monthly medical examinations but they may need regular supplies of drugs. For them to have to visit a doctor every week or two simply to obtain a prescription is clearly a waste of everyone's time. Doctors do not usually prescribe quantities of drugs likely to last more than four weeks since some drugs deteriorate if kept too long and most practitioners feel that it is unwise to allow any patient to keep excessively large quantities of drugs at home.

Unfortunately, repeat prescribing is not always restricted to patients with long–term problems requiring continuous medication. Patients who really should see a doctor (rather than simply continue taking tablets) sometimes ask for repeat prescriptions and, to the shame of the medical profession, not infrequently obtain them.

Many patients have become psychologically dependent upon sleeping tablets and tranquillisers because of the ease with which they have been able to obtain repeat prescriptions.

Arrangements for obtaining repeat prescriptions vary a good deal from one doctor's practice to another's. In some practices patients entitled to receive prescriptions are issued with cards on which the drugs which they are allowed to receive without any consultation are listed. There may be a limit on the number of prescriptions which the patient may obtain without being reviewed. In other practices the cards detailing drugs which can be provided on repeat prescriptions are kept with the patient's notes so that the receptionists, who usually write out repeat prescriptions, can check on drugs, and dosages, and make a note of the number of prescriptions used.

Theoretically, doctors signing prescriptions should check all the details, including specific points such as the dosages and quantities of drugs to be supplied, and general points such as the suitability of continuing with the treatment. In practice, many repeat prescriptions are signed with few or no checks being made. I have, in the past, obtained evidence showing that some doctors sign piles of virgin prescription forms and leave their receptionists to fill in the blanks. I have little doubt that this practice continues.

I suggest that patients receiving drugs on repeat prescriptions should always check that the tablets they receive match the tablets previously prescribed, and that any instructions on the bottle label match previous instructions. If there is any confusion or uncertainty then a telephone call should be made to the surgery.

As a general rule, I suggest that only patients who have established long–term clinical problems should obtain drugs on repeat prescriptions and they should visit the surgery at least once every six months to check that the medication does not need changing. Patients with short–term or acute conditions who need medication should always speak to a doctor.

Repeat prescriptions can be a convenience. But they can lead to drug misuse and eventual abuse – and to addiction and dependence. They can also lead to death.

67. I have learned that patients improve their chances of benefiting from a drug – and they also minimise the risk of problems – if they know what to expect (and if they understand what side effects they should expect).

You have a right to know what you are taking – and why. Don't be shy. Here are some questions you should ask your doctor:

1. What is this medicine for?

2. How long should I take it? Should I take it until the bottle is empty or until my symptoms have gone?

3. What should I do if I miss a dose?

4. What side effects should I particularly watch out for? Will the medicine make me drowsy?

5. Am I likely to need to take more when these have gone? Should I arrange another consultation?

6. Are there any foods I should avoid? Should I avoid alcohol? Should I take the medicine before, with or after meals?

7. How long will the medicine take to work – and how will I know that it is working?

Whenever your doctor gives you a drug to take it is vitally important that you watch out for side effects. Four out of ten people who are given drugs by their doctors will suffer uncomfortable, hazardous or even lethal side effects.

Drugs which are highly promoted when they are launched, but which are eventually shown to be totally useless, often cause illnesses far worse than the complaint for which they were prescribed. Far more people are killed by prescription drugs than are killed by illegal drugs such as heroin and cocaine. And as I have pointed out on many occasions no less than one in six hospital patients are there because they have been made ill by their doctor.

Perhaps the most convincing evidence of the failure of our current drug testing systems to protect patients lies in the number of drugs which have had to be withdrawn after they have been passed as 'safe' by the authorities. I know of over 80 drugs which have had to be withdrawn or restricted because they were considered to be too dangerous for widespread use. Some of these drugs were withdrawn after months. Others were taken off the market after being sold for years.

Can you imagine the outcry if testing methods were so inadequate that 80 types of motor car or 80 varieties of food had to be withdrawn because they were found to be unsafe?

Doctors, the drug industry and the Government all claim that nothing can be done to avoid this drug scandal. I don't believe this is true. If governments really wanted to protect patients there are many things they could do.

Since the end of the 1970's, I have argued that we need an international, computerised drug monitoring service – designed to make sure that doctors in one part of the world know when doctors in other countries have spotted problems. Astonishingly, no such system exists.

You might imagine that when a drug is withdrawn in one country other countries will take similar action. But you would be wrong. One drug that was officially withdrawn from the market in the USA and France was not officially withdrawn in the UK until five years later!

I believe that one of the main reasons for the international epidemic of drug–induced illness is the greed of the big international drug companies. They make a fortune out of making and selling drugs and their ruthlessness and levels of profit make the arms industry look like a church charity.

Governments could dramatically reduce the incidence of lethal, dangerous and uncomfortable side effects by insisting that drugs be extensively tested before being prescribed for millions of people around the world. At the moment drugs can be launched onto the mass market after relatively few tests have been done. The authorities admit that they don't know what side effects will be produced until a drug has been on the market for a while.

And patients would be far, far safer if drug companies were stopped from testing drugs on animals. Pharmaceutical companies love to test drugs on animals because they can't lose. If the animal tests show that the drug doesn't produce side effects in animals the company will proclaim the drug 'safe' and put it on the market. But if the animal tests show that the drug causes side effects the company will dismiss the results as irrelevant – and put the drug on the market anyway – 'because animals are different to people'.

If you have ever suffered unpleasant side effects the chances are high that the drug you were given was tested on animals. The evidence available now shows that animal experiments are so misleading and inaccurate that they result in many human deaths.

Despite the fact that one must hold the pharmaceutical industry directly responsible for most of the side effects (and deaths) caused by drugs there is no doubt that the number of problems could be reduced if patients were more aware of how best to protect themselves from side effects.

It is a sad but true fact that of all the drugs prescribed only a relatively small number are taken in the way that the prescriber originally intended them to be taken. Drugs are taken at the wrong time, they are taken too frequently and they are sometimes never taken out of the bottle at all.

It is important to remember that modern prescribed drugs are not only potentially effective but also powerful and potentially dangerous.

Here are some tips to help you minimise your risk of developing a side effect if you have to take a prescription drug.

- Some drugs can be stopped when symptoms cease. Others need to be taken as a complete course. A small number of drugs need to be taken continuously and a second prescription will have to be obtained before the first supply has run out. The patient who knows what his drug is for, why he is taking it and what the effect should be, will be more likely to know when a drug is to be stopped.

- If a drug has to be taken once a day, it is usually important that it is taken at the same time each day. If a drug has to be taken twice a day it should usually be taken at intervals of 12 hours. A drug that needs to be taken three times a day should usually be taken at eight–hourly intervals and a drug that needs to be taken four times a day should usually be taken at six–hourly intervals. The day should be divided into suitable segments.

- Some drugs which may cause stomach problems are safer when taken with meals. Other drugs may not be absorbed properly if taken with food.

- A number of patients (particularly the elderly) are expected to remember to take dozens of pills a day. When a day's medication includes tablets to be taken twice daily, three times daily, mornings only and every four hours, mistakes are inevitable. If a patient needs to take a number of drugs a day mistakes can be minimised by preparing a daily chart on which the names and times of different drugs are marked. Such a chart will reduce the risk of a patient taking one dose twice or struggling to remember whether a particular pill has been taken yet.

- To avoid the risk of overdosage sleeping tablets should not be kept by the bedside. It is too easy for a half–asleep patient to mistakenly take extra tablets. In the case of a suspected overdose medical attention must be sought.

- Always follow any specific instructions that you have been given by your doctor. Read the label on your bottle of pills and take notice of what it says!

- When you're not using them drugs should be stored in a locked cupboard out of reach of children, in a room where the temperature will be fairly stable. The bathroom is probably the worst room in the house for storing medicines. Your bedroom – which probably has a more stable temperature – is much better.

- Never take drugs which were prescribed for someone else. Return all unused supplies of drugs to your pharmacist.

- It is wise to assume that all prescribed drugs can cause drowsiness. You shouldn't drive or operate machinery after taking a drug until you are sure that you are safe.

- Drugs do not mix well with alcohol. If you want to drink while taking drugs ask your doctor whether or not it will be safe.

- Do not take non–prescribed medicines while taking prescribed drugs unless your doctor has told you that you can.

- Do not stop taking drugs suddenly if you have been advised to take a full course. Ring your doctor for advice if you need to stop for any reason. Some drugs have to be stopped gradually rather than abruptly.

- Be on the look out for side effects and remember Coleman's First Law of Medicine: if you seem to develop new symptoms while taking a prescription drug then the chances are high that the new symptoms were caused by the treatment you are taking for your original symptoms.

- Report any side effects to your doctor – and ask him if he's going to report the side effects to the authorities. The vast majority of doctors never bother to report side effects – with the result that potentially hazardous drugs remain on the market for far longer than they should.

- If you need to see a doctor while taking a drug make sure he knows what you are taking – particularly if he intends to prescribe new treatment for you. Many drugs do not mix well together and may, indeed, react together in a dangerous way.

- Do not assume that a doctor you have seen in the past will remember what he prescribed for you on a previous occasion.

- Learn the names and purposes of the drugs you take. If you are not sure when to take the drugs that you have been given ask your doctor or the pharmacist. If you think you will forget the instructions you are given ask for them to be written down. The name of the drug should always appear on the container.

- Do not remove drugs from their proper containers except when you need them or if you are transferring them to a device intended to improve compliance.

- Try to see the same doctor as often as possible. If several doctors are prescribing for you there may be an increased risk of an interaction between drugs which do not mix well.

- Use drugs with care, but do use them when they are required. Doctors sometimes divide patients into two main groups: those who are willing to take drugs for any little symptom and who feel deprived if not offered a pharmacological solution to every ailment, and those who are unwilling to take drugs under any circumstances. Try not to fall into either of these extreme groups.

68. I have learned that it is important that patients do not allow their doctors to label them.

If, a few years ago, you went to see your doctor complaining that you felt miserable he would have probably prescribed a harmless tonic, chatted to you for twenty minutes and told you to try and get out and enjoy yourself a bit more.

Today, if you go to see your doctor and complain that you feel under the weather he will probably diagnose you as suffering from depression. There is an excellent chance that he will then start you on one of the many new powerful chemicals now available.

Until recently depression was a fairly uncommon disease.

But today depression is one of the fastest growing diseases in the world. And the boom in the diagnosis of depression has coincided with the development of special, new, expensive, chemical anti–depressants.

My fear is that the diagnosis of 'depression' is now often being made when patients are simply unhappy or generally fed up with their lives. And some of the new anti–depressant drugs may, I fear, prove to produce dangerous or nasty side effects.

It may well be true that a relatively small number of depressed patients can be helped by taking drugs.

But I believe that the amount of good that is being done by these powerful drugs could be far outweighed by the possible harm.

I have absolutely no doubt that there is more unhappiness in our society than there has ever been in any previous society but I strongly suspect that many of the patients diagnosed as suffering from 'depression' may well be 'sad' (and suffering from the toxic stress disorder which I call The Twenty First Century Blues) rather than clinically 'depressed', and may need help of a different kind.

I believe that instead of automatically dosing all their unhappy patients with powerful and potentially hazardous chemicals, and attempting to tackle a vague and ill–defined disease, doctors should be encouraging more of the sad, the despairing and the unhappy to try to tackle the specific causes of their unhappiness themselves. It can be done.

Depression is not the only disease which is said to be commoner today than it used to be.

Asthma is another disorder which is often said to affect more people now than in the past.

And arthritis is a third disease which is alleged to be getting commoner.

In my view the problem is not that these (and many other) diseases are necessarily becoming commoner, but that doctors are diagnosing them more often and more readily.

Take a mild wheeze into a doctor's surgery these days and the chances are that the doctor will tell you that you have asthma and that you must use an inhaler for the rest of your life.

Complain of an aching joint and you'll be labelled 'arthritic' – and given pills to take for the rest of your life.

As a result of this wild over–prescribing policy countless thousands of people who regard themselves as asthmatics, or arthritics are nothing of the sort. They have, in truth, merely exhibited minor, temporary symptoms which do not need long–term treatment.

The driving force behind this vast over–prescribing is, in my opinion, the ubiquitous drugs industry.

The drug companies want doctors to prescribe more medicines (for the simple reason that prescribing more pills pushes up profits even higher) and it is, I believe, their subtle, ever present, overall, global influence which results in doctors deciding that every wheeze must be treated as asthma, that every ache must be diagnosed and treated as 'arthritis' and that every mild bout of unhappiness must be treated as depression.

Diseases such as asthma, arthritis and depression are perfect for making big profits because patients labelled as suffering from these conditions are often advised to take pills for years or even decades. It is by no means unusual for patients to be told that they need drug therapy for life. And with pills often costing a small fortune the profits on each new patient can be colossal.

This bizarre, ruthless but profitable philosophy works because doctors are usually far too ready to listen to the drug company salesmen. These days most doctors are actually taught about new drugs not by independent experts but by paid salesmen.

My advice is simple: if your doctor tells you that you are suffering from a long–term disorder for which you need to take long–term drug therapy – you should ask for a second opinion.

Never forget that four out of ten patients who take pills suffer side effects. If you are taking pills because you genuinely need them then the risks may be acceptable. But if you are taking pills unnecessarily then the risks are unnecessary too.

69. I have learned that in nine out of ten illnesses my body can and will heal itself. (And that this is true for your body too.)

Many of the people who are injured by doctors never needed medical treatment in the first place. The human body contains a comprehensive variety of self–healing mechanisms which mean that in nine out of ten illnesses your body will mend itself.

It is important that you learn to understand your body; learn to appreciate your own self–healing skills; learn to acknowledge your body's miraculous range of techniques for dealing with threats and diseases; and learn to know when your body can look after itself – and when you need professional help.

The big trouble with most health care professionals – and this includes acupuncturists, osteopaths, aromatherapists and all other 'alternative' practitioners, as well as orthodox doctors – is that they tend to treat their patients as battle grounds, the illness as an enemy and their own armoury of drugs or techniques as weapons with which to fight the illness.

Whether he sticks needles into you, gives you herbal tea to drink or prescribes a drug for you to swallow the therapist has to do something to you, or give you something to take, in order to justify his fee.

The evidence to show that this interventionist philosophy is wrong is incontrovertible. When you fall ill you do not necessarily need to have anything done to you. Your body is equipped with such an enormous range of subtle and sophisticated feedback mechanisms that it can look after itself very well.

Your body can heal itself, protect itself and guard itself against a thousand different types of threat.

Your body contains internal mechanisms designed to deal automatically with minor damage, improve your eyesight, keep out the cold, deal with anxiety and even help fight against diseases as threatening as cancer.

Your internal appetite control centre can ensure that you eat only the foods that your body needs – and it can help make sure that you never become overweight.

Your body's internal pain–relieving hormones are as powerful as morphine – but you have to know how to take advantage of those pain–relieving hormones.

The human brain even contains a natural drug designed to help anxiety.

Your body is marvellous. It contains a vast variety of extraordinarily effective self–healing mechanisms. Most of them you probably don't even know about. And if you don't know about them then you probably don't know how to take advantage of them.

Your body cannot always cope, of course. There will be times when even your sophisticated self–healing mechanisms will be overwhelmed and will need support.

But to dismiss these mechanisms on the grounds that they don't provide a complete answer to all health problems is like arguing that it isn't worthwhile learning to swim because occasionally you may need the help of a lifeguard.

I firmly believe that if you learn to use the power of your own body you will benefit in a number of ways.

First, of course, you will reduce the risk of being injured by a healthcare professional. Every year thousands of people suffer because of unnecessary treatments used by orthodox and alternative practitioners.

Second, you will benefit because when an interventionist treats an illness he usually tries to oppose your body's own internal responses, as well as whatever outside agent may have triggered those responses in the first place. This isn't necessarily a good idea. All symptoms are merely signs that a fight is taking place inside your body. Unless the interventionist treatment is carefully designed to support and aid your body, the treatment applied may well end up damaging and even weakening your body's internal mechanisms – eventually making you more vulnerable and more reliant on interventionists and their treatments.

It is vitally important that you learn to use your body's powers and learn to recognise precisely when you need professional support. You should retain overall control of your body and bring in the healers as advisers and technicians.

Once you've mastered the idea of using your body's own healing powers you will find yourself enjoying a freedom that you might otherwise never know.

I have described the many wonderful ways in which your body can look after itself in my book called *Bodypower*. The book explains how you can use your body's self–healing powers to help you deal with 9 out of 10 illnesses without a doctor. It has been described as the owner's manual for the human body.

70. I have learned that it is possible to use simple tricks to manipulate people in authority.

Bank managers, doctors, tax inspectors and others use their desks to establish their authority. They sit behind them and use them as barriers – to establish their superiority. I know of one doctor who used to shave the bottoms off the front legs of the chair in which his patients sat. Because they were constantly sliding forwards, patients always felt slightly uncomfortable – and never wanted to stay too long.

When you visit the surgery and your doctor waves you to a chair a couple of feet in front of his desk he is putting you in an exposed and vulnerable situation. He possesses the desk and is defended by its bulk. You sit alone with your personal space unprotected.

But, as I showed in my book *People Watching* it is very easy to reverse the situation and take control. When you enter the surgery move the chair a few inches so that it is closer to the desk. Then sit down so that you can lean forward and put your elbows on the desk. If there is a letter rack in front of you gently but firmly move it to one side. Put your hat, gloves, newspaper, shopping, handbag or notebook down on the desk. If your doctor is leaning forwards to establish his territorial rights over his desk he will almost certainly respond by leaning backwards and abandoning his control of the desk. His response will be automatic. You will then be able to start your consultation in a much stronger position. You will be in charge of the consultation – a much safer position from which to seek advice.

71. I have learned that if I make my voice heard I will feel better.

We live in a world where cruelty is honoured, where dishonesty is rewarded, where kindness is taken for weakness, where power is taken by the vicious and the brutal and where the inept, the incompetent and the uncaring prosper.

We live in a world where integrity is sneered at, where honesty is described as controversy, where passion is regarded as an embarrassment and where the truth is a dangerous commodity.

We are ruled by pompous authoritarians who cloak their petty ambitions and personal greed in stolen power and glory but accept no responsibility for justice; today, the million horsemen of the Apocalypse gallop ever onwards in malignant determination to destroy truth, honesty and compassion.

Morals and ethics have become abstract subjects for university debate, rather than guidelines for our behaviour. Our leaders no longer care about what is right. Those in authority no longer care about the poor, the meek, the gentle and the kind. They do not care about the innocent.

Our society cares only about what is regarded as proper and 'normal'. The joy of giving is an object of scorn and derision. Nobility and honour are freely bought and sold.

We have dirtied our land and polluted our air and our water. We live in a filth of our own making; a filth that gets worse each day and which contaminates our very lives.

The establishment applauds and rewards the fat businessmen who cheat the world's poor. We are encouraged by our leaders and the media to kneel before the representatives of evil and daily pledge our allegiance to witless, passionless mediocrity.

We are taught to treat those with whom we share this planet with idle, rough, contempt. We use them for our own ends without a thought for their comfort, happiness or dignity.

And yet we claim to be innocents in all this corruption of the spirit. We blame an unseen 'them' for the horrors of our world. We blame 'them' for the cruelty, the viciousness and the misery. We live in comfort and contentment; slumped in front of the TV screen; deaf to the injustices which mark our world.

It is a slick trick we play on ourselves.

For we have built this society. It is our responsibility. We cannot escape from blame by keeping silent. The evil that is done is done on our account and if we stay silent it is done with our blessing.

Remember, then, that it is up to us to shout 'stop' when we have had enough of the wickedness around us.

If we want to change things we must campaign and protest and not rest until our voices are heard. If we do nothing then we are just a silent part of the evil which is corrupting and destroying our world. And we can change things.

For example, I first started my campaign to warn doctors and patients about the dangers of overprescribing benzodiazepine tranquillisers back in 1973. For ten years the only thing the campaign produced was a fairly constant stream of personal abuse – much of it from doctors who were offended that anyone should dare question the medical establishment. Editors who supported my campaign were reminded that most doctors disagreed with me. Because of my constant campaigning about tranquillisers I was always in trouble. Numerous doctors publicly claimed that the benzodiazepines were perfectly safe – and that I was irresponsible to frighten the public with articles, books and broadcasts about these drugs.

By the early 1980's, after ten years of campaigning, a growing number of doctors finally agreed that I was right. Gradually, as the campaign grew, many other journalists and broadcasters joined in the battle. Whereas I had originally been a lone voice – and therefore relatively easy to dismiss – those defending the widespread use of benzodiazepine tranquillisers and sleeping tablets found themselves on the defensive. In 1988, the Government in Britain finally took action – admitting that they had done so directly because of my articles. A fifteen year campaign had been vindicated. But it still took several more years before doctors really changed their prescribing habits.

Today there cannot be more than a handful of patients or doctors in the world who do not accept that these drugs can be addictive – and need to be used with extreme caution.

The benzodiazepine campaign was exhausting, expensive and time consuming – but it is clear from this battle that you and I do have power; we can change things. But we must fight together. Doctors and politicians responded to the benzodiazepine campaign when the protests could no longer be ignored. The lesson is that we must be persistent and determined.

If you care about the world in which you live and want it to be a better, safer place for humans and animals then you must make your voice heard. Don't worry if people scoff or mock. Don't allow yourself to be put off by scorn, derision, undisguised contempt or a lack of support or encouragement from others.

Just remember that imaginative, thoughtful and creative individuals have always had a hard time. Look back in history and you will find countless examples of citizens who were harassed or persecuted simply because they dared to think for themselves – and tried to share their thoughts with others.

Our world has never welcomed the original, the challenging, the inspirational or the passionate and has always preferred the characterless to the thought-provoking. Those who dare to speak out against the establishment have always been regarded as dangerous heretics. The iconoclast has never been a welcome figure in any age.

Confucius, the Chinese philosopher, was dismissed by his political masters and his books were burned. Those who didn't burn his books within 30 days were branded and condemned to forced labour. Two and a half thousand years later Confucius's influence was still considered so dangerous that Chairman Mao banned his works.

Described by the Delphic Oracle as the wisest man in the world, Greek teacher Socrates was accused of corrupting the youth of Athens, arrested for being an evildoer and 'a person showing curiosity, searching into things under the earth and above the heaven and teaching all this to others'. Socrates was condemned to death.

Dante, the Italian poet, was banished from Florence and condemned to be burnt at the stake if ever captured.

After they had failed to silence him with threats and bribes the Jewish authorities excommunicated Spinoza in Amsterdam because he refused to toe the party line, refused to think what other people told him he must think and insisted on maintaining his intellectual independence. He and his work were denounced as 'forged in Hell by a renegade Jew and the devil'.

Galileo, the seventeenth century Italian mathematician, astrologer and scientist got into terrible trouble with the all powerful Church for daring to support Copernicus, who had the temerity to claim that the planets revolved around the sun.

Aureolus Philippus Theophrastus Bombastus von Hohenheim (known to his chums as Paracelsus) made himself enemies all over Europe because he tried to revolutionise medicine in the sixteenth century. Paracelsus was the greatest influence on medical thinking since Hippocrates but the establishment regarded him as a trouble-maker.

Ignaz Semmelweiss, the Austrian obstetrician who recognised that puerperal fever was caused by doctors' dirty habits was ostracised by the medical profession for daring to criticise practical procedures.

Henry David Thoreau, surely the kindest, wisest philosopher who has ever lived, was imprisoned for sticking to his ideals.

Original thinkers and people who do not fit neatly into the scheme of things have never gone down well. And nothing has changed. Today, incompetence and mediocrity thrive and are now subsidised, supported and encouraged by our increasingly bureaucratic and intrusive society. Schoolteachers and social workers encourage mediocrity because they themselves are mediocre. Talent frightens them witless. Among bureaucrats and administrators incompetence and mediocrity are esteemed virtues; these be–suited morons revere the banal and worship the bland.

The unusual or the eccentric attract scorn and ridicule. Politicians are frightened of anything new or challenging. They reject the innovative, the creative and the imaginative in favour of the accustomed, the comfortable and the ordinary. It is hardly surprising that the sensitive, the thoughtful, the imaginative and the caring find 21st century life almost too painful to bear.

If you feel that something is wrong, and you feel passionately that something ought to be done about it, then stand up for your principles, shout and make your voice heard. There is a chance that some people will regard you as a lunatic. I have no doubt that many small–minded people will sneer and tell you that in trying to change the world and root out dishonesty, corruption and injustice you are tilting at windmills. But there is also a chance that your voice will be heard; that others will respond and that you will win your battle. And the benefits of victory surely far outweigh the insults of the insignificant. Only when you've found something you are prepared to die for will you really know what life is all about.

72. I have learned that I can provide myself with some protection against viruses.

If you think that viruses are just wishy washy bugs that cause flu, tummy upsets and other relatively minor inconveniences – think again. Viruses are now a major threat to your health – and your family's health.

Consider the Ebola virus, for example. It can kill in days. There is no cure. The illness starts with a headache and a fever. Just like flu. Within days blood starts to seep from every orifice. And the body rapidly starts to deteriorate. Every organ fails. Just a virus.

There are three main reasons why viruses are becoming increasingly dangerous.

First, international air travel means that killer bugs can be taken from one country to another within hours. There was far less danger when infected individuals travelled on slower forms of transport. Patients carrying the disease would have died long before they reached heavily populated cities.

Second, viruses are constantly changing – and getting stronger. As scientists produce new vaccines existing viruses adapt and change.

Third, vivisectors in laboratories around the world are constantly giving existing viruses to animals. They use some of the rarest and most deadly viruses in their experiments. Some of the research work is done for the military – who want ever more lethal viruses for biological warfare. Problems really start when viruses – or infected animals – escape from laboratories.

There are countless billions of viruses in the world – each is one thousandth the size of a bacterium. Every one could be a ticking time bomb.

But here is what you can do to help protect yourself and your family from killer viruses:

1. Spend as little time as you can in crowded places. The more people there are the more likely it is that there are lots of viruses around.

2. Campaign for all animal experiments to be stopped at once. Laboratory experiments on animals are a major cause both of the development and the release into the community of deadly new viruses.

3. Wash your hands frequently and thoroughly. The world is full of viruses. They are everywhere. And quite invisible to the naked eye. You can pick up a virus by shaking hands, picking up change in a shop or touching a door handle.

4. Don't share food or eat food from other people's plates.

5. Practise safe sex.

6. Avoid wild animals – and keep away from animals behaving in a peculiar fashion. If you are bitten by an animal get medical help straight away.

7. Teach children not to cough or sneeze without using a handkerchief.

8. Wash all kitchen dishes and cutlery thoroughly in hot, soapy water.

9. Try not touch your eyes with your fingers – that's an easy way for viruses to get into your body.

Those general rules will minimise your chances of being contaminated by a virus.

73. I have learned that it is important to know what money is for.

How much money do you need? And what do you need it for? How much do you want? And what do you want it for? Most investment books I have ever seen never even ask these questions. The authors seem to assume that acquiring money is an end in itself with no purpose necessary other than the accumulation of wealth. But these are the most important questions of all. (Needs and wants are, of course, very different. We all need food and shelter. No one needs a yacht. No one needs to own a football club. No one needs to own a diamond encrusted gold watch.)

None of us actually needs very much money.

It's the wanting that is special.

So, what do you want money for? Just for necessities? Helping others? Looking after yourself and your loved ones in the future when the State has thrown you on the scrapheap? Luxuries? Do you like travelling first class and enjoy eating expensive delicacies?

Do you want money because you know it will buy you freedom? Money doesn't just buy foods, shelter and clothing. It doesn't just buy electric nose hair clippers. Money also buys a certain amount of freedom. 'If someone tells me to do something I don't want to do I can say 'No' because of my money,' one actor explained.

If you want money then first you have to know what you want it for. There has to be a purpose. Otherwise you might as well be collecting blades of grass or old newspapers. Money doesn't have any value unless you do something with it. It can buy you a yacht. And it can buy you (or someone you love) medical treatment that might not otherwise be available. As far as I am concerned the one thing money can provide which I really value is freedom. Money gives me the freedom to write what I want to write and to make sure that it gets published and marketed without worrying too much about whether or not it is commercially successful. (In the bad old days most publishers used to operate like this. They published what they wanted to publish – regardless of whether or not it was likely to make money. If they were unlucky they went bust. If they were lucky they published enough commercially successful books to pay for the commercially unsuccessful books. So far, I'm pleased to say, I've managed to ensure that the commercially successful books I write make more than enough money to pay for the commercially unsuccessful books I wanted to write and publish anyway.)

And how much money do you really need?

Take a good hard look at your income and expenditure. Do you need more money for the things you want to do with your life? Or could it be that you already have enough income (and enough money saved up) to buy everything you need? Are you, perhaps, simply wasting money on things you neither want nor need. I know a fellow who lives in the country and has a job in the city. He spends six hours a day on trains (three hours each way) and an hour a day on the Underground. That is seven hours a day, five days a week. He says he has the benefit of a London salary while living in a large house in the country. But he spends seven hours a day travelling. Unless there are breakdowns, of course. When there are breakdowns he spends even more time travelling.

74. I have learned not to waste my life penny pinching.

You aren't going to get rich by buying cheap beans or cheap jam. And cheap doesn't necessarily save you money. Always figure in the value of your time. For example, if you are travelling somewhere and there's a choice of going by coach or train think about the time it's going to take you. Which journey will take longest? And will one form of transport enable you to do something useful while you are travelling? I can work on trains but I couldn't possibly work on a coach. I get travel sick on coaches and I can't get my long legs between the seats. If I travel by coach I risk getting a deep vein thrombosis and I waste the time I'm travelling. If I travel by train I can go in some comfort and I can work while I travel. The travelling time won't be wasted.

If you buy cheap, new furniture it will probably fall apart, it will never make you feel good and it will be worthless when you come to sell it. If you buy good, relatively expensive, old furniture it will not fall apart, it will make you feel good when you use it and if you ever want to sell it, it will probably be worth more than you paid for it. The same isn't quite true for clothes (you probably aren't going to be able to sell them at all) but good clothes will always look better, feel better, keep their shape better and last longer. And good clothes will make you feel good too. (There is the added bonus that when you are travelling, security guards and waiters will usually treat you better if you are well–dressed than they will if you are dressed in scruffy, cheap clothes. It's just human nature. They know that rich people are more likely to have clout and make their lives miserable if they mess them around too much.)

Buy quality, rather than quantity. And, remember: it isn't wrong to spend money on yourself occasionally. Enjoy your money. Enjoy making it. Enjoy having it. And enjoy spending it. What is it for if not to enjoy?

I have learned not to make false economies. I usually drive big cars. I keep them and drive them into the ground. There are several reasons for this. I like big cars because I'm tall and my back aches if I spend too long in a tiny car. I also like big, well–made cars because they tend to be tougher and give you a better chance of surviving a crash. I also prefer them because they tend to break down less often and usually last longer.

But I hate looking for and buying new cars. It's a tiresome, time consuming chore. One friend buys a new, small car every two years. He sniffily claims that his vehicles are much cheaper to run and better for the environment. He has to change these tinny little things after two years because by then they're not fit for anything much. The cars he buys are made out of some sort of plastic-coated reinforced cardboard and they fall apart if kept too long. His cars use less petrol than mine but I don't use my car all that much (I prefer to travel by train) so I don't spend much more on petrol than he does. His cars are cheaper to mend when they break down but they break down a lot more often. Bits are always falling off them and the dealer usually manages to find a clause in the contract which excludes the latest disaster from the guarantee.

So what's better for the environment – buying a big, expensive car which lasts or buying loads of smaller, cheaper cars which have to be replaced every couple of years? The slightly surprising truth is that the big, expensive car is much, much better for the environment.

75. I have learned that financial security is, to a certain extent, a state of mind.

Lots of people think that having a job with a big company provides more security than working for yourself. It is true that the self–employed have less immediate security. They often don't know where the next job is coming from. But in a downturn big companies often lay off employees. No one can make you redundant if you are self–employed. You may find it harder to get work, and you may have to work longer hours for the same income as before, but you aren't going to be queuing on the docks waiting for a chance to unload ships.

Financial security means knowing that whatever happens you and your family won't starve because you will be able to find a way to earn a living and put bread on the table. I know a millionaire who keeps a bicycle, a ladder and a bucket in his garage next to his Rolls Royce and his wife's Mercedes sports car. 'If I lose all my money,' he told me once, 'I'll start a window cleaning round and build it up again.' The bicycle, the bucket and the ladder are his ultimate financial security.

Having some savings will provide you with security against bad times, misfortune and mistakes.

But do not trust anyone to look after your financial security blanket for you. Do not trust banks. Do not trust brokers. Do not trust advisers. And, most of all, do not trust the Government or any official regulators. The financial world today is riddled with regulations which make life difficult for everyone. The regulations will not, I fear, protect you against thievery, dishonesty or incompetence. The bottom line is that there is no one more interested in your financial security than you are.

76. I have learned that it is easy to accumulate stuff I don't need. And I have learned that much of that stuff will cost me a great deal in terms of time and energy.

Look around your house. How much stuff have you got that you don't need? How much time and energy are you wasting looking after it and providing storage space for it? How much time are you wasting looking at and wondering if you'll ever wear it again, find the manual or find the other bit that makes it work? How much of it could you sell? How much of it could you give away to your local charity shop? How much of it should you throw away? How much cleaner – and clearer – will your life be without all this unnecessary stuff?

Few people need a new car every two years. Most people have more pairs of shoes than they really need. Millions have electrical equipment they never use. Standard of living and quality of life aren't the same thing but we confuse the two.

There have been more shopping malls than high schools in the USA for many years. Three quarters of people who go shopping are not looking for something in particular. They are simply out 'shopping'.

We all need to get into the habit of asking ourselves why we buy the things we buy. This isn't a judgemental question. But it's a question well worth asking. How many jumpers do you really need? Why do so many people insist on having an entirely new outfit if they are planning to attend someone else's wedding? The complaint 'I don't have a thing to wear' has become a joke.

I know a handyman who earns his living painting, bricklaying and doing bits of carpentry. He's a real jack–of–all–trades and he's very good at what he does. But it's difficult to get him to come and do anything because he only works two or three days a week. The rest of the time he messes around on his boat or in his garden.

A few months ago I asked him why he didn't work harder.

He explained that he didn't see any point in earning more money than he needed to satisfy his fairly simple needs. He told me that he has paid off his mortgage, that although old and rather battered his car is his own and that he has all the furniture he wants. He has, he told me, managed to put aside a few hundred pounds in the building society for emergencies.

I asked him if his wife was happy with this philosophical approach to employment. He said that she was very happy and that they spent much of the week gardening together, walking along the cliffs or, on sunny days, bobbing around in their little boat. He also told me that he and his wife don't have holidays away from home because for them home is a pretty constant holiday but that they do spend a day every month travelling to demonstrations against hunting, vivisection and other examples of cruelty to animals.

He also told me that because his earnings are low he pays hardly any income tax.

I found his attitude enormously refreshing. This local handyman is leading the life of a true revolutionary. I suspect that Henry David Thoreau, the philosopher of Walden Pond, would have been proud of him.

Before you dismiss the handyman's lifestyle as impractical ask yourself how much of your life you spend earning money to buy things you don't really need and are only buying to impress people you don't really care about.

Here's a simple little exercise you can try.

Make a list of everything other than food that you've bought in the last year. By the side of each item on your list make a note of the price you paid.

Then divide your after tax annual income by the number of hours you work to find out how much you earn an hour. Don't forget to deduct any essential business expenses from your income before you do this calculation.

Now you can easily use this figure to find out how long you had to work to buy each of the items on your first list.

I have learned that knowing how much I earn per hour is extremely useful.

Get into the habit of thinking of the things you buy in terms of hours rather than pounds.

If you buy a television set that costs £1,000 and you earn £10 an hour then the television set has cost you 100 hours.

If you buy a book for £10 and your income is £10 an hour then the book has cost you one hour.

Every time you spend money ask yourself how long you have had to work to pay for it.

How much of your life are you giving in order to buy a car with a three speed rear window wiper instead of one with a one speed rear window wiper? (That was the sole difference between two models of a car I once considered buying. The extra price was £500.)

This can be a frightening exercise for you'll quickly realise that you've given a great deal of your life in order to buy junk that you don't really need.

Add up the cost of all the unnecessary stuff you bought last year and work out how much of your life you wasted earning money to buy stuff that hasn't improved or changed your life.

The whole point of modern advertising is to persuade people to buy things they don't need; to turn shallow wants into desperate 'must haves'.

It is skilful advertising which encourages otherwise sane people to spend a fortune on double glazing which will never pay for itself and to spend thousands of pounds ripping out a perfectly serviceable kitchen and replacing it with another slightly different kitchen.

And, of course, the more money you have to earn to buy all this stuff that you don't really need the more income tax you will have had to pay.

If you are happy with the things the Government buys with your money then you won't mind giving them great chunks of it. But are you really happy with what they do with it?

I'm not suggesting that the handyman's life style is right for everyone.

But you might like to think about all this a little.

We live in a society which encourages the accumulation of goods: a smart, shiny motor car; a beautiful home; a wardrobe full of expensive, beautifully designed clothes – these are what we are encouraged to work towards.

If you are not careful the stuff you think you own could end up owning you. Our world has been taken over by a lot of materialistic, acquisitive nonsense. We buy coffee table books that no one ever reads, fancy toilet roll holders, lotions to make fat thighs thin, creams to make small breasts melon–sized and to make melon–sized breasts positively breathtaking and all sorts of other nonsenses. We buy things for the sake of buying. We buy presents that are neither beautiful nor useful.

Do not allow material possessions, belongings of any kind, to take over your life. Next time you are buying something other than an everyday item ask yourself if you are making the purchase because you want it or need it or because you have been persuaded to buy it by someone else – or, worse still, by Society. And then remember how many hours you have to work to earn that item.

And regularly take time to go through all your possessions and sort out those which you want to keep and those that you neither want nor need to keep. 'Spring–cleaning' your possessions has several advantages. It will enable you to see exactly what you have (you may be surprised to discover things you had forgotten you owned) and it will also enable you to convert unwanted items into cash. You will have more space available and you will be able to find and use the belongings which are left more easily and more effectively. Clear out the stuff you own at regular intervals and throw away everything which doesn't add value to your life. If you haven't used something or worn something for six or twelve months sell it or give it to a charity shop.

And always remember William Morris's advice: 'Have nothing in your home that you do not know to be useful or believe to be beautiful.'

77. I have learned that during the last few hundred years we have changed our world much faster than our bodies have managed to evolve.

That's why we suffer so much from stress related diseases. We still have bodies designed to cope with the sort of threat posed by sabre toothed tigers but we live in a world where our stresses come in brown envelopes and land on our doormats every day. It isn't our fault that we suffer more from stress than anyone in history. I have learned that in order to cope we have to reduce our exposure to unnecessary stresses, we need to know how to relax and we need to make time in our lives to rest, relax and recharge our worn–out batteries.

78. I have learned to be careful not to buy too much insurance.

The extended warranties so beloved by electrical stores are a perfect example of the way fear is used to sell us expensive products we probably don't really need. The small print is usually complicated and far too daunting to read in the time available. And so we hand over another substantial sum for an over–expensive extended warranty. (The fact that many stores now make a considerable portion of their profit from selling these warranties should tell you something about their value to the customer.)

We have been brought up willing to pay to avoid risk. And some risks (the big ones) are always worth insuring against. Most of us need to take out public liability insurance because if a slate falls off our roof and lands on a passer–by the resulting claim for damages could bankrupt us. Most of us need to insure our homes against fire because if our house burns down we won't be able to afford another one. This sort of insurance doesn't usually cost a great deal (because the risks are quite small) but it is worth buying.

But much of the insurance we are sold doesn't fit into that sort of category. Most of the time we insure ourselves against losses which will not seriously embarrass us. To make things worse we take out extra insurance when the manufacturer's guarantee will protect us against the risk of buying a particularly shoddy item. And our excessive zeal for insurance cover means that we end up buying multiple cover for the same risks. The expense of these accumulated policies can be horrendous.

The variety of risks against which one can now take out insurance is apparently unending. Every time you buy one insurance policy the company from which you bought it will try to sell you another policy, covering areas that weren't included in the first policy. The small print invariably means that the insurance company can find an escape clause or a reason to charge another fee for something else.

We should really only insure against losses that we really cannot afford – huge legal costs for example. For the rest, most of us – particularly those who are careful and honest – will probably be better off if we put the premiums into a special savings account and use that to pay for plumbing costs, heating repairs and so on.

And since it is probably not worthwhile making a claim against an insurance policy unless the claim is considerable, it makes sense to agree formally not to make a claim for small sums, in return for a discount on the premium. (Remember, too, that insurance companies now tend to put up premiums when they pay out. A small claim can lead to an annual rise in premiums which matches the one–off payment.)

The careful and honest lose out twice in the current way of things. First, they must pay high premiums to include the cost of all the false claims that will be made and the cost of all the problems which will arise because of poor maintenance or bad habits. Second, they must struggle to obtain payment and then put up with small print clauses which exclude most claims and put huge excesses on the ones which are (eventually and grudgingly) paid.

Remember that insurance companies are routinely dishonest. They lie. A lot. When they tell you the cheque is in the post they are probably lying. When they tell you that the claims form is in the post they are probably lying. When they tell you that your claim is being processed they are probably lying. Insurance companies lie (and make life exceedingly difficult for anyone trying to make a claim) for one very good reason: they hope that if they make things difficult for you then you will get bored and go away without them ever having to fork out.

I have never taken out insurance against ill health. There are two reasons for this. First, I try to look after my health. This means that if I pay premiums to a medical insurance company I will be subsidising all the over–weight, meat–eating smokers who don't take any exercise but do need a lot of medical attention. Second, I long ago worked out that if I put money aside each month I could use that money if I fell ill and needed private treatment. The money I've put aside has been earning its keep for years. On the other hand, premiums paid are lost for ever. (I have, however, always had a sickness policy that pays me money for life if I am too sick to be able to work again.)

79. I have learned not to be frightened of, or bullied by, tax collectors.

'No man in the country is under the slightest obligation, moral or other, so to arrange his legal relations to his business or property as to enable the Inland Revenue to put the largest possible shovel in his stores,' said Law Lord, Lord Clyde. 'The Inland Revenue is not slow – and quite rightly – to take every advantage which is open to it under the Taxing Statutes for the purpose of depleting the taxpayer's pocket. And the taxpayer is in like manner entitled to be astute to prevent, so far as he honestly can, the depletion of his means by the Inland Revenue.'

It is our individual responsibility, as defined by law, to ensure that we pay as little tax as possible. That is our responsibility to our families and ourselves. 'Every man is entitled, if he can, to order his affairs so that the tax attaching under the appropriate Act is less than it would otherwise be,' said Lord Tomlin. An American judge, Judge Learned Hand, of the US Appeals Court, said something similar: 'There is nothing sinister in so arranging one's affairs as to keep taxes as low as possible. Everybody does so, rich or poor; all do right. Nobody owes any public duty to pay more than the law demands; taxes are enforced extractions, not voluntary contributions.'

Governments, however, don't always see things quite that way. As far as they are concerned what is ours is theirs and what is theirs is also theirs. Today, tax collectors around the world treat all taxpayers as guilty until proven innocent. Governments have bought stolen information to help their investigations; merrily ignoring the fact that if ordinary citizens did this they would be sent to prison for receiving stolen goods.

Here are some thoughts on tax and tax inspectors.

1. Don't bother trying to become a tax exile. Don't bother moving to a tax haven. And don't bother trying to avoid paying tax by becoming a PT (Permanent Traveller). Lots of people do this. But they spend time and effort and money in avoiding tax and they end up living in places that no one in his right mind would want to call home. Some years ago I seriously contemplated moving to Monaco. I found, to my astonishment, that it really isn't as straightforward as you might think. And Monaco itself is as dull and uninspiring as a council estate. It's full of tower blocks into which are crammed thousands of miserable tax exiles. The streets may be safe (Monaco has nearly as many CCTV cameras as Britain but they do at least use them to catch the guilty and protect the innocent rather than to simply pick up unfortunate folk who have parked in the wrong place or dropped litter into the wrong receptacle) but I am willing to pay not to live there.

2. Stay alert for retrospective tax legislation. The British Government has begun introducing retrospective legislation and is also using its tax collecting agencies to criminalise many civil activities. The result must surely be that people will be sent to prison for things that weren't illegal when they

did them, and will be handed huge and unexpected tax bills for earnings and profits that were acquired in the past. Things are likely to get worse rather than better. EU legislation, often gold–plated by an enthusiastically compliant UK Government, will make things ever worse.

3. Don't make an investment because of the tax break.

4. I am scrupulously honest on my tax form. The tax people spot check self–employed people quite often. They've investigated me twice so far. Both were full, year long investigations. And at the end of both I ended up getting money back from the taxman. I prefer it that way. Like most people who are self–employed I have enough crises and problems in my life without having to worry about the tax people. I like to know that if they investigate me then, at the end, I'm going to be the one getting a cheque.

5. I have learned to keep full financial records. The more bits of paper you have the more you are likely to be able to win against the taxman. On the last occasion that I was investigated I delivered the requested records crammed into a large suitcase.

6. Part of any appreciated asset belongs to the Government, so they share the loot when you're making a profit. But the Government shares the pain when you're making a loss. So, consider the taxman as a partner who puts up no money but shares your profits and losses. I regard the taxman as operating a protection racket. I give him money and in return he doesn't use violence against me.

7. Don't overestimate the intelligence of people working for the tax authorities. A few years ago I held a bond run by the bank Goldman Sachs. A payment from the bond was listed on the bank statement under the abbreviated heading 'Gold Sacs'. During one of its typically lengthy but pointless enquiries into my affairs the tax office wrote to my accountant telling him that they now knew that I was dealing in gold. Puzzled, he wrote back and asked them for more information. 'Your client is buying and selling sacks of gold,' replied the taxman, drawing attention to the reference to 'Gold Sacs' as evidence.

8. If you become even remotely rich you will attract the attention of the tax people. This is widely believed to be because tax inspectors now get bonuses for every pound they gouge out of taxpayers. It is clearly easier and more profitable to target the rich rather than the poor, and it is easier to get money out of the honest rather than the crooked.

9. Always understand your own accounts. For years and years I used an accountant who used to tell me how much I owed the taxman. I simply did what I was told and wrote out the cheques. One year, back in the mid 1990's, I followed his instructions and wrote out a cheque for £129,000 for my half yearly tax bill. Only when the taxman subsequently did a spot check on my accounts did it turn out that I'd paid several thousand

pounds too much. I got a welcome refund cheque. I fired my accountant who told me that it wasn't his fault. He said it wasn't his firm's fault either. His explanation was that his assistant had 'been using out–of–date textbooks'. I'd been paying this guy and his firm thousands of pounds for years. It seemed to me that the least they could have done was buy some up–to–date textbooks. So I got rid of him and decided to fill in my tax form myself. It's a real pain and it wastes a lot of time (though if I used an accountant I would still have to spend some time pulling together bits of paper to show him) but at any one time of the year I now know what I owe and when I've got to pay it. There are no more surprises. I like it better this way.

80. I have learned that much of what other people call progress isn't really progress at all.

Progress brings complications and complications take away our freedom. 'We were the first to assert that the more complicated the forms of civilisation, the more restricted the freedom of the individual must become,' said Benito Mussolini, the inventor of fascism and the spiritual father of the European Union.

My computer printer broke down. I wanted it repaired. But the dealer told me that it was two years old and out–of–date. Is that progress? My portable telephone needed a new battery. The company from which I bought the telephone just over a year ago told me that the telephone is no longer being manufactured. And they have also stopped manufacturing the batteries. This means that the telephone is useless and will have to be thrown away. Is that progress? I wanted to listen to some old–fashioned vinyl records. I tried to buy a record player. The assistants in local shops laughed at me when I told them what I wanted. Is that progress? The glass in the wing mirror on my car cracked. A few years ago, the garage would have simply replaced the glass. It would have taken a few minutes and cost very little. But the garage couldn't obtain a replacement glass. They had to send away for a sealed unit. The whole operation took weeks and cost a small fortune. Is that progress?

When I dare to ask what the hell is so terrific about progress, and why we have to bow before it as though it were the god of our times, folk 'tut tut' and look at me as though I'm an alien from another planet.

'You can't stand in the way of progress!' they say, implying that it would be improper, unpatriotic, immoral and probably illegal even to try.

Well, I've had enough of progress. Without progress everyone would still be in work. Without progress the workshops of the world would still be alive, men would still be making things they were proud of and it would be possible to buy things on a Wednesday and expect them still to be capable of doing whatever it was they were bought to do on Saturday.

There is a myth that progress means automatically 'better'. It doesn't. In reality, progress means that more and more people have to exchange a rich, varied, wholesome, healthy lifestyle for one which is hollow and filled with despair and loneliness. Progress means deprivation for people but strength for our administrative structures. Progress means that the jobs people do become more boring and less satisfying. Progress means more power to machines. Progress means that things are more likely to go wrong. Progress means more destruction, more misery and more tedium. Progress means more damage to our planet.

Those who worship at the altar of progress make two simple but vital errors. They assume that man must take full advantage of every new development and invention. And they assume that he must always search for a better way of tackling everything he does.

Neither of these two assumptions is soundly based.

Just because man invents computers, supersonic jets and atomic bombs he doesn't have to use these things. Those who believe implicitly in progress believe that we must always endeavour to use every new nugget of information we obtain. They believe that if man invents a quicker and more effective way to kill people then we must use this quicker and more effective weapon of destruction.

Progress-lovers believe that if it is possible to make a computer-controlled machine which manufactures identical galumps at the rate of 6,000 an hour then we must have that machine. And that those galumps will be better than galumps which have been hand carved by craftsmen.

The lovers of progress are so keen to embrace the future and eradicate the past that they will introduce new laws ensuring that only the new computer–made galumps can be sold. The market for the old–fashioned galumps will disappear.

The progress-lovers don't care about the fact that their galump making machine will put thousands of craftsmen out of work.

Progress for the sake of progress often simply means change for the sake of change. But change is not always for the better.

The problem lies largely with the definition of the word 'better'.

What, exactly, does it mean?

Is a television set better than a radio or a good book?

Is a motor car better than a bicycle?

Is an aeroplane better than a yacht?

Are modern motor cars, equipped with electric windows and air–conditioning, better than ancient Rolls Royce motor cars equipped with neither of these facilities?

Is artificial turf better than real grass?

Is a poorly written, badly acted television situation comedy, which is in colour, better than movies such as Citizen Kane and Duck Soup which were made in black and white?

Are artificial flowers better than the real thing?

Too often progress simply means more frustration and more unhappiness.

It means that we become more dependent on one another and less capable of coping with the crises in our lives.

Progress means that when something goes wrong with the electricity supply your central heating boiler won't work. Progress means that it has become nigh on impossible to mend anything around the home without calling in an expert with a van full of tools. Even then he will probably tell you that he's got to send away for another part.

Progress means that when your windscreen wiper blade needs replacing you have to buy a new windscreen wiper system.

Progress means that when you want to buy a niplet you have to buy a blister pack of five which can only be opened with a kitchen knife, a screwdriver and a blowlamp.

What is going on? What are we doing to our world? Will people be wiser, happier and more contented when nuclear powered, seven speed nose hair clippers are finally available?

It would be stupid to claim that all progress is bad. Progress is neither good nor bad unless we make it so. Progress is good when we use it rather than when we allow it to rule our lives. But no longer are we allowed to choose between those aspects of progress which we think can be to our benefit and those which we suspect may be harmful. Our society wants constant progress and that is what it gets.

81. I have learned not to allow myself to drown in bad news.

In the old days our ancestors worried only about their relatives, friends and neighbours. People knew little about the outside world – and the outside world began probably twenty miles away in all directions. Now, we are told everything that happens to everyone, everywhere. There is always a tragedy somewhere in the world for us to worry about: a flood, an explosion, a tsunami, an earthquake, a shooting, an aeroplane crash, a murder. If you are a caring person, the constant barrage of disturbing news can be, well, disturbing. I have given up watching the TV news. And I only rarely buy newspapers. I no longer expose myself to a daily diet of misery. This is not because I am disinterested in the problems of the world – I fight for the things I believe in and I read enough news magazines and news agency summaries to know about the important things going on in the world. But I know that I can only cope with so much misery and sadness.

I protect myself because if I allowed myself to be subjected to a constant daily diet of misery and horror I would not be able to cope – or have the strength to fight for the things in which I believe.

I don't know whether there is any more violence or horror in the world today than there was five hundred years ago. I suspect not. But that is an academic and irrelevant question. The point is that modern communications methods make these horrors available to us all on an hourly basis. At any one time there are around forty wars going on around the world. All these wars – and the accompanying horrors – are brought into our homes through the magic of television.

Modern communications techniques mean that you and I receive more information every day than our ancestors had to cope with in years. Television gives us instant access to other people's pain.

Our brains are constantly hurrying to process information. When human beings are overexposed to information and stimulation they become anxious and, eventually, mentally ill.

When much of that information is depressing and disturbing the response is even faster.

Naturally, the more sensitive and thoughtful the individual the greater will be their potential susceptibility to this type of stress.

(The people who do cruel things do not feel bad about anything much. If they were the sort to feel bad they would not do the things they do. In our world the sensitive suffer for everyone while the ruthless simply go from strength to strength because they genuinely don't care and don't suffer.)

I believe that one of the reasons why so many people do not seem to care these days is that they are protecting themselves by deliberately staying aloof and not allowing themselves to respond to the world around them. People numb themselves and suppress their emotions in order to survive. They become unfeeling because they are overexposed to horror and they simply cannot cope. They close their eyes and their hearts to protect themselves (and because the horrors they see and hear about are endless they do not believe they can do anything that will make a difference).

Many people have become so immune to awful news that they need extremely strong stimulation to make them sit up and take notice.

The growth and popularity of documentaries and dramas based on violence, crime and miscellaneous horrors is a symptom of the new need for constant excitement and stimulation.

People who are unmoved by genuine tragedy are naturally unmoved by what they see on their TV screens – even if it includes real live human beings being arrested or being treated in hospital.

Television chat shows used to be vehicles for movie stars to tell engaging anecdotes; these days they are full of angry people talking without shame or embarrassment about their unhappy sex lives, sharing their hostility for their neighbours and blaming their parents for their misery.

And I have a suspicion that the popularity of realistic horror movies among young people these days is merely a sign of the fact that they have become immune to ordinary fears and terrors.

The horror movies that were popular a few decades ago would not frighten today's teenagers in the way that they frightened my generation.

Today's teenagers and children need new horrors to stimulate their deadened imaginations.

We feed our children a constant diet of horror, abuse and violence and then express surprise when they become violent themselves.

If you want to stay alert but sensitive to the world's problems then I suggest that you too limit your exposure to news programmes. Limiting your exposure to the daily diet of horror and injustice will enable you to retain the strength to do what you can to fight for truth and justice.

82. I have learned that it is important to buy organic food – food prepared without carcinogenic chemicals – whenever possible. (And I have learned to ignore the 'official' reports which tell me that it is a waste of money to do so.)

Nearly half of all the food sold in supermarkets and stores – including fruits, vegetables, bread and meat – contains potentially dangerous pesticide residues. Some chemicals are sprayed onto foods which are being picked or shipped to the stores but many chemicals are absorbed when foods are growing and obviously cannot be removed by washing or scraping. Some of the chemicals used by modern farmers are known to cause cancer, asthma and a wide variety of other serious disorders.

Meat is contaminated partly because of the chemicals which are given to animals (to keep them 'healthy' and to make them grow more speedily) and partly because of the chemicals which are put into or onto the food they eat.

Organic food is grown without the use of artificial fertilizers and pesticides and the extra money you have to pay for such food is extremely well spent. Organic farmers use natural fertilisers (such as animal manure and seaweed) and rely on natural biological pest controllers, though some use natural plant–based pesticides.

Moreover organic farmers also grow crops in rotation so that their soil is kept in good condition. Growing the same crop year after year in the same massive field probably makes good commercial sense but it means that the food produced will be lower in nutritional value.

Organic food is more expensive because farmers who use artificial fertilisers and chemicals to kill bugs, insects and infections can produce bigger, more reliable, more uniform, more predictable and more attractive looking crops. Organic farmers, who have to rely on growing food the way nature intended, tend to have smaller crops and they are more likely to lose their crop through disease.

When buying food and looking for organic produce you should check labels carefully and make sure that you find good, reliable local suppliers. Many organic farmers sell their produce direct to the public and in cities there are now many shops (and even some supermarkets) selling organic produce, either as an alternative to food grown with the aid of chemicals or alongside such produce.

I have learned that many of the people who so insistently tell us all that organic food isn't worth buying have a vested interest in promoting food that has been grown with the aid of chemicals.

83. I have learned that it is important to know what makes me happy – and that sometimes moments of happiness have to be planned.

Do you know what makes you happy? Do you know when you are happy? How many moments of happiness did you have last week?

You have to make time for happiness. You have to be ready for it. And you have to work at it.

When the good times come you have to make a real effort to enjoy them; to look around and take notice of the world so that you can savour and remember your happiness (and use it to keep you going when the times get rough).

Ask yourself these simple questions – you might find the answers illuminating.

What in your life gives you most fun? How much time do you spend doing it?

What in your life gives you most pain? How much time do you spend doing that?

Assess all the influences on your life and ask yourself how these things contribute to your life and potential for enjoyment and satisfaction.

Consider each influence and ask yourself: 'Should I discard it or give it more of my energy?'

84. I have learned that the most valuable commodity in the world is not gold, money or diamonds – but time.

You can't take minutes from tomorrow to replace those lost today. No one can give you back the minutes that have been wasted on petty nonsenses.

'Lost wealth may be replaced by industry, lost knowledge by study, lost health by temperance or medicine,' said Victorian author Samuel Smiles, 'but lost time is gone for ever.'

I had a telephone call from my friend J. He is a Zulu. He was on his way to Australia and called me from Bangkok. He told me that his plane had been delayed for nine hours.

'Oh, how awful!' I said, sympathetically. I always hate delays.

'What do you mean?' asked J. He sounded puzzled.

'The delay,' I explained. 'It must be awfully frustrating for you.'

'Not particularly,' replied J, sounding as ever calm, relaxed and unflustered. 'The delay is all part of the travelling. It is part of the experience. It means I have more time at the airport. I can read and talk and ring you.'

'But it's annoying to be so late,' I said.

'A few decades ago this journey would have taken me weeks,' replied J. 'What is nine hours?'

'Aren't you worried that you will be late for your meeting?' I asked him.

'The meeting cannot take place until I get there,' said J. 'How can I be late for it?'

Most people abhor waste. They squeeze the last few bits of toothpaste from the toothpaste tube, they use up scraps of soap and they scribble down thoughts and notes on the backs of old envelopes.

And yet most of us regularly waste something which is much more valuable than money: time.

Einstein may have proved that time is an illusion; malleable and fragile. But on a day to day basis time is important. And yet we waste it in a thousand different ways. We waste it gossiping. We waste it performing pointless and repetitive chores, many of which could be ignored completely. How many people in your life do you waste time with? How many of these relationships add value to your life? What do you offer to them that makes their lives better and what do they offer to you that makes your life better?

Wandering around in Paris recently I stopped in front of a complex window display involving mannequins, streamers and a hundred or so brightly coloured balloons. I haven't the faintest idea what the shop was selling. But the window display was terribly impressive. It must have taken days to design and put together.

A smartly dressed woman in her thirties was on her knees carefully dusting the balloons; meticulously wiping each tautly stretched rubber sphere with a damp cloth. The balloons weren't overtly 'dirty'. I'd walked past the shop a day or two earlier and the display hadn't been there then. But someone in authority had obviously been alarmed by the possibility that one or two of the balloons might have been defiled by a few specks of dust.

I felt deeply sorry for that woman in the shop window. It was, I felt, one of the most futile things I had ever seen anyone doing.

I found myself imagining the conversation she might have with her husband when she got home that evening.

'What have you done today, love?' I imagined I heard her husband ask. 'How did your day go?'

'I am exhausted,' I heard her reply wearily, in a husky, sexy, French tobacco stained voice. 'I have been dusting balloons all day.'

How terribly sad. What an entirely pointless activity.

It may sound rather comical but, the truth is that we all do some balloon dusting. We waste valuable energy, hard earned money and irreplaceable time on activities which do nothing whatsoever to improve our lives or anyone else's life.

Take a good hard look at the way you've spent your time, money and energy during the last week.

Which activities are you proud of?

And which were simply a waste of time?

How much of your life do you spend 'dusting balloons'?

The simple truth is that time is worth much more than money and is far too valuable to waste. For your own sake fill your life with passion and determination and leave the balloons undusted. It is extraordinary to see just what you can do with those ignored and forgotten moments. (To paraphrase a well–known saying I cannot resist the temptation to point out that in order to look after the hours it is only necessary to look after the minutes).

Many men have learnt a language while travelling to work and numerous books have been written in the period while waiting for dinner to be served. One well–known authoress wrote her first book while working as a governess. She wrote only in the time she spent waiting for her charge to turn up for lessons. Stephenson (of rocket fame) taught himself mathematics while working as an engineman during nightshifts. In his meal breaks he would work out sums. He used a piece of chalk for a pen and the side of a colliery wagon for a blackboard. Dr Darwin wrote down the thoughts which immortalised him while travelling from house to house in the country and Dr Mason Good translated Lucretius while riding in his carriage and visiting his patients around the streets of London.

I don't know whether it is still there but there used to be a message on the clock dial at a college in Oxford, England which read 'The hours perish and are laid to our charge'.

Just think for a moment what you could do if you had an extra hour every day of your life. And yet the chances are that you could easily find another hour a day – simply by cutting out waste. Do a little time and motion study on your life and see just where the minutes and the hours get frittered away. Take a cool, hard look at the way you waste your time doing things that really don't matter very much at all. The time spent (or rather wasted) on daily chores and rituals can quickly add up.

Assuming that you start at 20 and live to be 75 you will:

- Waste a total of 17 weeks if you spend 1 hour a week cleaning the car. (Why not let it stay dirty?)

- Waste a total of 34 weeks if you spend 2 hours a week cutting the lawn. (Let the grass grow and turn your garden into a wildlife reserve.)

- Waste a total of 40 days and nights if you spend 20 minutes a week ironing socks. (Why bother to iron socks?)

- Waste a total of well over 3 years if you spend 10 hours a week sitting in traffic jams. (Is your job really worth sacrificing so much of your life? Can't you find work nearer to home?)

- Waste a total of 836 days and nights of your life if you spend one hour a day Hoovering and dusting. (Hoover and dust for one hour a week instead of one hour a day and you will, effectively gain 716 days – that's equivalent to living an extra two years.)

- Waste a total of 3,345 days and nights of your life if you spend four hours a day watching TV. Cut your TV watching in half and you'll have an extra 239 weeks in which to do other things. That's like living for more than another four years. Although 'self improvement' is today widely despised by the pseudo intellectuals, you could learn a foreign language, write a book and become skilled at a favourite sport in that time.

85. I have learned that we all have to have a purpose for living.

A strong man without direction can be defeated by a child who has purpose.

People who have no real purpose in their lives quickly become bored and weary.

The rich who choose not to work often become desperately unhappy. Some simply drink too much. Others try to convince themselves (and others) that their dilettante charitable works are giving their lives meaning.

Lottery winners who are unable to adjust their minds to the new possibilities their wealth offers them often end up going back to their humdrum pre–wealth jobs in order to escape the boredom they feel.

Passion and purpose are vital. Without them life is meaningless. Moderation is not a virtue. Remember that it matters not how you live and die, but why you live and die.

Most people go through their lives without ever finding a purpose or without ever defining a plan. They get what they settle for. They never know what they want to do – or why. Their lives are governed by a series of accidents. They choose courses at school simply because their friends are doing those courses – or because they like the teachers. They choose jobs because they are convenient. They go through their lives with no sense of direction, no realistic hopes or expectations and no sense of purpose. It is hardly surprising that they constantly feel disappointed and frustrated.

Find what you want to do – and then do it the way you want to do it. Find, know and then be constant to your purpose in life. Set your own goals and define your aims and objectives. Decide what you want out of life and then make sure that you're going in the right direction.

Look around and you will see the passionless many, chilled of hope and overflowing with superficial responsibilities.

You can do better with your life.

You must decide what you want out of life because without purpose there can be no passion or drive. And remember that only when you have found a cause (or several causes) worth dying for will you really know the joy of living.

86. I have learned not to believe everything I read, see or hear.

History is not necessarily what happened. History is, to a very large extent, simply what has been reported as having happened. History – and the 'truth' – are what people believe and remember. History – whether it be personal, national or international – is made up of memories, interpretations, feelings and prejudices rather than the original facts. We do not remember what happened so much as what we think happened and how we responded to what we think happened.

All this is important because it means that our knowledge and understanding of our personal, national and global history depends very much upon the way we appreciate and respond to the facts of our personal, national and global experiences.

Since the way we 'see' and 'hear' the news depends very much upon our knowledge and our past experiences, it is clear that if we are to form a lucid view of the world (in all its aspects) we need to be presented with reliable, trustworthy information.

This does not happen. It is now almost impossible to get hold of trustworthy news about significant events through the normal media. Most people think they get the truth by reading, listening to and watching newspapers and radio and television news programmes. Sadly, however, they don't get the truth: they get what the editors want them to read. Editors and journalists are these days increasingly likely to run corporate press releases as news stories. (It's quicker and cheaper than researching news stories and far less likely to produce lawsuits or controversy.)

Several decades ago I revealed that some medical magazines were accepting 'advertising' as editorial. Today, at least one newspaper has been found guilty of doing this. It is simply no longer possible to buy a newspaper and expect to have an honest understanding of what is going on in the world when you have read it.

If you buy all the newspapers and news magazines available on any one day you will see different stories, different emphasis, different facts and different interpretations – within the stories which are supposed to be 'news' stories. A story which hits the headlines in one paper might not appear in any other papers at all.

We are, in practice, fed a rich diet of lies, half truths and propaganda. Newspapers, radio stations and television stations are usually either government controlled or dependent upon advertisers. Many are little more than parts of show business. In order to stay in business they have to sell their product. If they don't attract readers, listeners and viewers by making sure that their presentation of the news is exciting and 'sexy' they will lose money and go out of business.

Crowds either destroy or worship the object of their attention. And they can turn on a whim. The individual who is, at one moment, a hero can easily become a villain. Newspapers are much like crowds. They can turn a villain into a hero or a hero into a villain in the printing of a page. A journalist friend once told me a story which illustrated this fact well. Late one day the newspaper for which he worked received a story about an ordinary man who had done something to attract public attention. The details of the story are irrelevant. The newspaper's first inclination was to turn the man into a hero. They planned to publish a photograph and a story drawing the attention to the wonderful thing this man had done. But as they planned their story another story came into the newsroom. And the individual who was at the centre of this story was even more of a hero than the first person. And so, because the newspaper did not want to have two heroes on its pages, the editors turned the first man into a villain. A man who had, a moment or two earlier, been a hero in waiting now became a villain in waiting. He was attacked and vilified for doing the very same things for which, a moment or two earlier, they had been planning to praise him. And a man's life was ruined simply so that the newspaper editors could 'balance' the stories on their pages. Remember this next time you read any newspaper story. Depending upon the way in which it is written virtually any individual can be described as both a hero and a villain. Today's newspapers are merely comics for grown–ups.

All around the world those who read broadsheet (as opposed to tabloid) newspapers are rather naively convinced that they are getting the real facts. Sadly, this simply isn't true. The broadsheets publish exactly the same gossip and pre–packaged public relations fodder as everyone else. Indeed, the tabloids usually offer a more honest approach to most issues. There are two reasons for this. First, the journalists working for tabloid newspapers are of an infinitely higher quality. It is quite common for broadsheet journalists, columnists and contributors to 'graduate' to writing for a tabloid – where the pay is invariably much better – but almost unheard of for a tabloid journalist, columnist or contributor to take the step down to a broadsheet. Second, because tabloid newspapers tend to sell far more copies than broadsheets – and earn a considerable part of their income from the cover price – the publishers are usually less susceptible to pressure from advertisers than are the proprietors of broadsheet newspapers. Broadsheet publishers are less likely than tabloid editors to be prepared to annoy any large, powerful, rich companies. Finally, because they have acres of space to fill, and are therefore more likely to end up reprinting news releases and information handouts, broadsheets are, like television news programmes, a lobbyists dream.

Most mass–market news reporting, whether published in tabloid newspapers, broadsheet newspapers or magazines, or broadcast on the wireless or on television, is now biased and prejudiced. That wouldn't matter so much if the bias was open and the prejudice was visible. But the bias is frequently covert and the prejudice is rarely open. Those with vested interests to support (for example, the food industry and the drug industry) construct theories to support what they do and systematically and deliberately stimulate and encourage existing fears and prejudices which are to their advantage. Journalists then obediently and politely regurgitate these prejudices as though they were fact.

Today, all mechanisms for spreading information are used almost exclusively to spread views which, true or false, will strengthen a belief in the rightness of decisions taken by those in authority. Information that could cause doubt is withheld or suppressed. Every time you read a story in a newspaper or see a news programme on television you should ask yourself 'Who did that story benefit?' 'Why did they tell me that?' Acquire and nurture a healthy suspicion about the news media.

Those who write and speak on behalf of the fascists and totalitarians ensure that language is perverted. Words are changed so that meanings are hidden. Propaganda destroys the morals of the people because it undermines the basic foundation of all moral values – the truth. And the sad end result is that people often do not feel oppressed because they are thinking as they were taught to think – they do not see anything wrong in the world around them. They do not think for themselves because they have not been taught to think for themselves and it is does not occur to them that they are entitled to think for themselves.

There are many influences which determine the extent, depth and direction of bias and prejudice in the media.

Some, such as the influence from advertisers ('If you publish/broadcast that story we will pull our advertising') is often direct, simple in operation and easy to understand.

Some, such as the influence from proprietors, shareholders and owners is rather more subtle but just as dangerous and certainly just as (if not more) effective. The proprietor or company chairman who has a global operation and who is hoping to do a deal with a government in one part of the world is unlikely to be pleased if one of his newspapers or television stations elsewhere in the world publishes an attack on that same government. Wise editors and producers make it their business to know the deals their proprietors and company bosses are involved in – the hidden agendas which they must take care to respect – for they know that if they are too 'independent' they will simply find themselves being replaced. (In order to avoid a public outcry this is usually done by promoting the individual who has transgressed to some superior position which sounds impressive and carries a large salary but has no editorial power. Within a few months the individual concerned can be eased out into the cold.)

Television is almost certainly the weakest and most unreliable source of information – and yet it is to television that most people turn when they want the 'facts'. People feel comfortable with the television. They trust it because they can look at the pictures and think that they are seeing what is happening. And yet television is, generally speaking, pretentious, precious, self–congratulatory and superficial. An ability to smile and banter, bouffant hair, capped teeth and a certain sexual chemistry with a colleague are infinitely more important than irrelevant old–fashioned nonsenses such as a respect for truth and justice. Like radio, television is constrained by the fact that every story must be read out aloud. This means that a fifteen minute bulletin is unlikely to contain more than around 1,000 words of text. And that means compacting and summarising world events in a way which inevitably distorts. A television or radio news programme will contain far fewer words than a page or two in a tabloid newspaper.

It is its very dependence upon pictures which is television's main weakness. Because there are often no pictures of major news items (there clearly cannot possibly be a camera crew on hand whenever an embassy is stormed, a riot starts, an aeroplane crashes or a road accident occurs) the television team in the studio usually has two alternatives: either to use film and pictures taken from their library (often without saying that the film is stock footage taken some time earlier) or to adapt the news priorities to fit the available pictures – demoting in the running order the story of the demonstration in China or the earthquake in India and leading the news bulletin with the pre–arranged event for which there is fresh, new film.

Most of the film stories television stations show have been arranged in advance. If the TV crew is there, and filming, it is almost certainly because their editor sent them there. And he or she sent them there because the news team received an invitation. Television is the public relations officer's dream, the lobbyist's perfect medium. A television news programme can be played like a piano. The lobbyist or public relations officer thinks up a good film opportunity, invites the TV crews and sits back and waits for the little bit of luck which is needed to ensure that his item gets a good showing on the programme.

People who work in television do their very best to hide all the truth about their own shortcomings from the public. They will frequently run stories complaining about the way in which newspapers (particularly the tabloid newspapers) have dealt with a story when in practice their own method of dealing with the story has been every bit as intrusive, one–sided and unfair as the tabloid treatment. I have seen television programmes complaining about press intrusion which have shown a crowd of press photographers and described them as ghouls. Neither the television news teams nor the viewers seem to have identified the television cameraman, sound man and the rest of the film crew as being part of the rabble.

It is much easier to distort the truth on television than in just about any other medium. By holding the camera on an interviewee for a long period of time or by switching the camera to the interviewee in an unguarded moment it is possible to give a totally misleading impression of the interviewee. And if all else fails it is easy enough to edit out the interviewee's wise, sound, sensible or witty responses and keep in only the dull, inarticulate or stumbling remarks. If that still doesn't satisfy the requirements of the editor or producer, or the vanity of the presenter, it is quite easy to cut in some sharp, cutting or incisive remarks from the interviewer at a later stage. Anyone who appears on a recorded television programme must inevitably trust the integrity of the television team.

Viewers tend to forget that television is primarily an entertainment medium.

You will probably not be surprised to hear that, in my view, books, preferably published by small, thoroughly independent publishers, are now the most reliable, independent source of information and news.

But the growing number of genuinely independent newsletters which are now published and distributed throughout the world are also an excellent source of independent and reliable information about world, business and commercial affairs. The editors (often also the publishers and owners) of these newsletters usually have no paymasters other than their subscribers. They have no advertisers and no corporate responsibilities. They are frequently passionate and prejudiced but their passions and prejudices show and are not hidden. By subscribing to more than one of these newsletters it is possible to obtain a much greater insight into what is going on in the world than by reading daily newspapers or watching the television news.

87. I have learned that most people eat a terrible diet.

The first problem is that we have changed the type of food we eat faster than our bodies have been able to adapt.

We were designed (or slowly evolved) for a very different type of diet to the one most of us eat today. We were designed for a diet based on fruits and vegetables, supplemented occasionally with a small amount of lean meat. We weren't designed to eat vast quantities of fatty meat and we weren't designed to drink milk taken from another animal (and meant for its young).

Around 99.99% of our genetic material was formed when we were eating that sort of diet. But now most of us live on fatty meat, milky foods and cereals.

There were 100,000 generations of humans known as hunter–gatherers (living on fruits and vegetables they gathered and animals they occasionally managed to kill) and 500 generations dependent on agriculture (living on food grown on farms and animals reared in captivity).

There have been just ten generations of humans since the onset of the industrial age and just two generations have grown up with highly processed fast, junk food.

In an attempt to stay healthy most of us want to eat nutritious, healthy food that tastes good and does us good. We want to be able to pay a fair price for food that contains natural ingredients and, ideally, no chemical residues. If the food we are buying contains additives we would like to know what they are.

In order to make sure that we do our best to eat healthily we naturally put a lot of faith in the labels used to describe the food we eat.

Our faith is misplaced.

Encouraged and supported by governments, food companies lie, lie and lie again. Ordinary, everyday words such as 'fresh', 'natural', 'wholesome' and 'nutritious' are virtually meaningless.

Food companies are aware of our desire for genuinely good food and so they employ clever advertising and marketing 'spin doctors' to help disguise the way that the food they sell us is adulterated by behind–the–scene chemists.

If doctors told their patients the truth about food most of the world's drug companies would virtually disappear within months. The market for heart drugs, high blood pressure drugs, anti–cancer drugs and so on would fall through the floor. Drug companies would be struggling along side by side with the buggy whip manufacturers.

And yet the advice about nutrition given to patients by doctors, nurses, nutritionists and dieticians is often appalling and frequently lethal. The food served in hospitals (where people are, it can safely be assumed, at their weakest and at their greatest need of wholesome, nutritious food) is almost universally inedible and customarily harmful to the patient. The food produced for patients is nothing more than unwholesome stodge, full of calories and fat and devoid of vitamins. You're more likely to find salmonella or staphylococci in a plateful of hospital food than you are to find a vitamin.

Knowing all this it is hardly surprising that most of us are ill most of the time.

A healthy diet contains a good, regular supply of fruit and vegetables. Simple.

88. I have learned to take risks (but to calculate the odds first).

The saddest words in any language are: 'If only...', 'It might have been...' and 'I wonder what would have happened if...'.

Make two lists. On the first list write down all the errors you have committed and which you now regret; the mistakes you know that you have made and which you now wish you could have avoided. On the second list write down all the errors of omission you have made; the things you haven't done but which you now wish you had done.

Whichever list is the longer will tell you a great deal about yourself – and will, perhaps, give you a hint about how you should conduct your life in the future.

If your first list is the longest then maybe you are being a little reckless – and taking too many risks. But if the second list is the longest (and many people are surprised to find that this is the case) then you should perhaps be taking more risks.

Most of us regard risk taking as both hazardous and unnecessary. And many people would say that they try to avoid risks whenever they can. Some people probably seriously believe that they are wise in constantly doing all they can to eradicate risk from their lives.

But taking risks is a necessary and unavoidable part of life. Every decision worth making is potentially dangerous. There is a risk in every venture you undertake – personal, professional or commercial.

Every time you get out of bed or walk out of your home you are taking a risk. Every time you make an investment you are taking a risk. (Despite words such as 'guaranteed' there is no such thing as a safe investment. Even a government bond can be risky if the government falls.) Every time you begin a new relationship or a new business project you are taking a risk. It is impossible to live without taking risks.

But what you can do is to make an attempt to quantify the risks before beginning any new venture. Only when you have quantified the risks can you make a sound judgement about whether or not an individual risk is worth taking. You must put risks into perspective. I know of a man who takes vitamin supplements because he believes that the vitamin will help reduce his risk of developing cancer. But he smokes heavily. If he really wants to reduce his cancer risk he would be much better advised to stop smoking.

One of the great tragedies of life is that we tend to take fewer risks as we get older. We become more wary of danger and more aware of the things that can go wrong. The danger is that a preoccupation with safety may reduce the possibility of success.

We should take more – not less – risks as we get older. After all, as we age we have less to lose. Regularity, habit and commonsense tend to paralyse. But not taking risks is, paradoxically, sometimes the most dangerous option.

You should learn to take risks which have the highest possible upside and the lowest possible downside. In order to succeed you have to be able to assess risks accurately. You should learn from your own mistakes but (and this is just as important) you should also learn from other people's mistakes.

Knowing the bottom line leads to confidence which leads to success.

89. I have learned how important it is that food is prepared and cooked carefully to reduce the risk of infection and to preserve the nutritional content.

Your body's immune system needs supplies of vitamins and minerals in order to function effectively. In particular, in order to help build up your immune system and fight off infections and cancer your body needs regular, good supplies of foods which contain anti–oxidants (beta carotene, vitamin C and vitamin E) and other substances.

The modern 'meat, butter, cheese, milk' diet is death to your body's immune system not just because those foods are rich in fat but also because they don't contain much in the way of immune boosting vitamins and minerals.

The healthiest, safest, most efficient and most effective way to obtain the vitamins and minerals you need is to get them from the food you eat. If you eat a good diet you won't have to worry about Recommended Daily Allowances or which sort of supplements to buy.

Your body will get the vitamins and minerals it needs to keep your immune system healthy if you eat a diet which is rich in vegetables, fruits and grains.

However, it is vital to be aware that vitamins can easily be destroyed. Mushrooms, lettuce, broccoli, asparagus and strawberries, for example, all lose their vitamins very quickly. Food which has to be cooked should be cooked for the shortest possible time and at the lowest possible temperature. In order to ensure that the food you eat retains a high vitamin content − and to minimise the risk of acquiring an infection from your food − you should follow these simple rules:

1. Food processing tends to reduce the nutritional quality of food and so where possible you should try to buy fresh food and either eat it raw (if appropriate) or eat it after cooking for the shortest length of time. (And all food should, of course, be thoroughly washed before eating.)

2. Buy vegetables whole. Don't have the leaves removed from carrots or the stalk removed from a cabbage or cauliflower. If you buy the vegetable whole vitamin C will continue to be produced and moved into the edible parts of the plant.

3. Cook foods in the minimum amount of water or steam.

4. Avoid high cooking temperatures and long heat exposure.

5. Do not allow food to stand for long periods at room temperature. Do not store food in warm places.

6. Do not soak vegetables for long periods.

7. Do not peel fruit or vegetables unless necessary. (For example, do not peel apples or skin potatoes).

8. Try to use food the day you have bought it.

9. You can keep fresh products for longer by freezing as soon as you buy them. Deep freezing preserves vitamins and other nutrients. Vegetables should be blanched before freezing. Put them in hot water for a short time. This inactivates enzymes which might otherwise degrade vitamin C.

10. Do not allow food − particularly un−packaged fruit and vegetables, vegetable oils and milk − to stand in sunlight.

11. Make sure that your fridge is kept cold enough. The temperature inside your fridge should be below 3 degrees Centigrade.

12. Make sure that you wash your hands thoroughly before preparing food. Staphylococcus, for example, can be transmitted hand to hand.

13. Never refreeze food which has been previously frozen and then thawed. Thawing increases the number of bacteria and refreezing food increases the chances of infection.

14. If you eat meat make sure that it is completely thawed before you start to cook it. If you do not do this then the chances are that the middle of the meat will still be frozen when you start to cook it − and will not be properly cooked when the rest of the meat is ready. Meat which is raw will probably be full of bugs.

15. Keep foods apart from one another in your fridge in order to reduce the risk of cross contamination. If you eat meat (a high risk source of infection) then put it at the bottom of the fridge and keep it away from other foods.

16. Don't ever buy tins which are rusty, bulging or badly damaged.

90. I have learned that it is sometimes wisest to do nothing.

This is often difficult to do and may require some strength of will.

91. I have learned to use my imagination and my subconscious mind.

'It doesn't matter where you live,' said Henry David Thoreau, 'where you live is really in your head.'

You must develop and use your imaginative skills.

Most people are unimaginative. This is not because they do not have any imaginative skills but because they do not know how to use them. Many may be frightened of displaying any imagination.

When in prime condition you can use your imagination to rework and rearrange old ideas, to see potential where there is no apparent hope and to discover ways through when there seems to be an impasse. You can also use your imagination to create new ideas out of thin air. Newton, when he was asked how he had produced his great discoveries replied: 'I keep the subject continually before me and wait till the first dawnings open slowly little by little into a full and clear light.'

If you allow your imagination to develop you will soon realise that most of the things which most people regard as 'impossible' are not impossible at all. Eventually, you will come to regard the word 'impossible' as a challenge.

This will give you a tremendous advantage over all those people who think that the things you are planning to do are 'impossible'. Most people are far too aware of all the things which are impossible – and which they are convinced will not work. I suggest that you do not even allow the word 'impossible' to enter your mind. When deciding whether or not to do something ask yourself not: 'Is this impossible?' but 'Do I want to do this?' (And if you answer 'yes' to the second question use your imagination to help you decide how).

Your imagination has a far greater control over your life than you might realise. Put a piece of wood on the ground and try walking along it. Easy? Now, imagine that the piece of wood is suspended 1,000 feet above a swamp filled with alligators and try walking across it again. The more you can convince yourself that the piece of wood really is suspended above a swamp the more difficult you will find it to walk across.

Your imagination can work against you. But it can also work for you. You can use your imagination to help you achieve whatever you want. Create in your mind the idea of what you want. Hold the idea in your mind. Sum up what you want in a few words. Close your eyes and imagine yourself writing those words down on an imaginary blackboard.

Now think of all the relevant facts and information you have. Hold those facts in your mind. With your eyes still closed write down the facts and information on an imaginary blackboard. Then get on with something else.

When you think about your problem next you will find that your subconscious mind will have produced several possible answers.

If you have difficulty in getting your imagination to work then you should buy yourself a bundle of notebooks and a pile of pens and pencils. Use the pencils and notebooks to write down everything you think of – practical plans, thoughts, fears, hopes and ideas. Get into the habit of writing down everything which comes into your head. If you do this then you will free your mind and you will stimulate your imagination to work harder and more effectively.

Once you start carrying a notebook with you – and using it – you will have far more ideas than you can cope with!

Your imagination is the key to success. Your imagination is your mind's workshop. And your imagination will grow and develop the more you use it.

92. I have learned not to let people push me around.

Is there someone in your life who makes you feel inadequate? Your mother? Your boss? A sarcastic or manipulative friend? Do you know someone who always puts you down and makes you feel a loser? Such people can cause immense physical and mental distress – and even create illness.

Do you get pushed around a lot? Do you spend most of your time doing things that other people want you to do?

Are you spending your life the way you want to spend it? Are you spending your life with the people you want to be with – doing what you want to do?

To get the most out of your life you must be able to answer 'No' to the first two questions and 'Yes' to the second two questions.

Are you going in the right direction?

There are only three reasons to do anything: because it may improve the world for other people or animals; because it is fun; because it makes money.

Rate all the activities in your life for: fun, money, improving the world.

How will you spend next weekend? How much time will you spend doing things that you really want to do? And how much time will you spend doing things that you aren't looking forward to – but that other people want you to do?

Make two lists of how you're likely to spend your time.

On the first list put the things you're looking forward to – the things you'll enjoy.

On the second list put the things that you feel you ought to do, the things you think other people expect you to do and the things you're not looking forward to at all.

Put down everything: meals, TV programmes, visitors, parties, trips out, sports, chores.

Now see which list is longest.

If your second list is the longest then you need to stand up for yourself more and the chances are that you get pushed around a lot by just about everyone you know; friends, relatives and employers especially.

You probably do errands for people who could perfectly well do their own errands. You're probably the sort of person who gets lumbered with looking after the children while everyone else goes off to a party. You probably work overtime at a job you hate – without getting paid for it. You get the boring jobs when you're on a committee.

And you never dream of complaining when you get rotten service in shops and restaurants.

The chances are that you're too shy, too soft–hearted and too nice to complain or say 'no'. You don't stick up for yourself. And the chances are that your health is suffering.

I'm not suggesting that you try to turn yourself into a selfish bully.

But if you continue to allow other people to push you around – then the chances are that you'll not only end up physically and mentally worn out but you'll also become so frustrated, and acquire so much hidden anger and resentment, that you'll become physically ill.

Headaches, backache, eczema and indigestion are just four of the disorders you're most likely to suffer from.

Moreover, if you become ill then your tolerance for pain will be low and you'll take longer than you should to recover.

Learning how to assert yourself – and stick up for yourself – isn't difficult.

Here's my advice:

1. Remember that you're an individual and you have rights.
Of course you should try to help people who are less fortunate than you are. But don't let yourself be suckered into looking after people who can look after themselves. Thousands of mums spend their days acting as slaves for teenagers who could (and should) do more for themselves. You have a right to some fun in your life.

2. Stop apologising unnecessarily.
If you're always saying sorry and feeling guilty then people will for ever be taking advantage of you. Only say "sorry" when you really mean it. And remember: you're not responsible for what people think or believe. Your only responsibility

is to be honest and true to yourself. You can do no more than that.

3. Build up your self-confidence.

Make a list of your assets. I don't mean cash but the really important things like knowledge, accomplishments, memories and skills.

4. Disarm your critic by agreeing with him.

When someone says: 'Your hair is a mess' just reply: 'Yes, I know.' Don't apologise. Don't try to find excuses. Just take the wind out of their sails by agreeing with them.

5. Don't let people label you.

If someone tells you that you are always unreliable or disorganised give some examples which show that you are just the opposite. If a critic tries to stick a label on you just refuse to accept it. If you are told that: 'You're always late' point out that you are late sometimes – but who isn't – but that most or much of the time you aren't late. If someone says you're clumsy, simply deny it but refuse to get into an argument.

6. Force your critic to expand and clarify their criticism.

Ask the critic to tell you exactly what they want you to do. People who moan and criticise are often not very good at offering practical advice. Chances are that you will put them on the defensive – you will certainly take the sting out of their attack. If someone says that you are inefficient ask them to tell you what their problem is so that you can deal with it. Invite them to give you more examples and keep inviting them to give you more examples.

7. Stay calm.

However angry or irate your critic gets you should stay cool. Eventually, there is a good chance that your critic will lose his or her temper. You can then (if you wish) retaliate by asking him or her why he or she is so touchy.

8. Remember that most bullies are physical cowards.

Be physically assertive. I don't mean that you should hit your critics. But stand up to them. Look them in the eye. Invade their personal space. Most bullies (and this is particularly true of emotional bullies) are cowards. Move closer to them and they'll probably feel uncomfortable, back away – and back down. Don't raise your voice but keep it firm.

9. Walk away or put the telephone down.

Refuse to get involved in a distressing argument. You don't have to put up with abuse from anyone.

10. Don't spend time with people who annoy you, constantly put you down or make you feel guilty.

I used to have a friend who was always putting me down. I liked him but I didn't like the way he seemed to feel it necessary to be constantly critical. I don't see him any more. Why waste your life on people who make your life miserable? I don't care who it is – colleague, friend or close relative – if they make you unhappy cut them out of your life.

11. Ignore gratuitous advice.

Just because someone tells you to do this, or suggests that you do that, you don't have to react. Say 'thank you' and then ignore them and do exactly what you want to do. If people offer minor criticisms, insults or sarcastic comments just ignore them. Stand up for yourself – you'll be healthier. Learn how to deal with toxic people – and how to handle people who make your life miserable or who make you feel inadequate. People can only push you around if you let them.

93. I have learned to be ready to adapt and to be always ready for change (because whether I like it or not change is coming).

Many people spend much of their energy trying to be in total control of their lives; trying to clear their desks and to get everything (relationships, belongings, work) just right.

This is a recipe for constant unhappiness and frustration because every time you think you have got your world sorted out some outside influence will come bursting in to disrupt things and you will lose control again.

The only constant upon which we can all rely is that tomorrow will be different to today and when tomorrow becomes today then tomorrow will, once again, be different.

Make yourself constantly adaptable to change and you will be in a far better position to survive. The moment you think you know the future and are in control, the moment you feel secure, that is the moment when the clock starts ticking on the unseen, unidentified, unexpected time bomb that will shatter your peace of mind. The moment you start to feel content, fate will start to smile.

You will only ever be in control of your life when you accept that you cannot have control and that change is a normal and acceptable part of life.

94. I have learned to use technology, rather than letting it use me. (And I have learned that you don't have to use it, just because it's been invented.)

Instead of giving us more freedom and greater opportunities, and instead of reducing our stress and making life easier, new equipment, such as computers, often creates more stress and greater pressure. As the pace of society increases, joy becomes increasingly elusive. We have to seek it out by taking conscious control of our lives, our time, and our priorities.

For example, the computer has made it possible for us to communicate far more speedily. Before the introduction of e–mail it would take several days to move a letter or a document from one desk to another. Today the same letter or document can be moved from one desk to another within seconds.

The result is that the recipient is under great pressure to respond speedily.

And so, in the end, everyone communicates far more frequently than they did before.

But the increase in the amount of communicating does not automatically result in an increase in the amount of profitable (in all senses of the word) endeavour. Creative (or profitable) work is constantly interrupted by trivial or meaningless e–mails. To avoid disappointing our correspondents, we feel that we have to stop what we are doing and reply to them.

Technology doesn't make life easier, it just makes life faster. Technology enables us to do more things and it enables us to do them more speedily but it doesn't enable us to do them better, easier or with more style. Because they are badly designed (by people who think they are brighter than they are) and oversold (by greedy people who are competing in a market which has traditionally put innovation above efficiency) computers will always do less than they are supposed to do. And they will always do it reluctantly and moodily.

Most of us are surrounded by labour saving gadgets which add to our daily stress rather than reducing it. Worse still, we often allow those gadgets to dominate our lives and our thinking. Telephones, fax machines and computers bring messages to us so quickly that we feel we must attend to them immediately.

But why should you always rush to answer the telephone or fax when it is inconvenient to do so, or when you really want to rest and relax? How many times in your life is it truly essential to produce an immediate response?

Many gadgets are expensive, complicated and unreliable. We fall for them because we believe they will make our lives easier. But often they do just the opposite.

Take a close look at every facet of your life. Throw out the gadgets which are more trouble than they are worth. Try not to bring equipment from work into your home area. And don't allow any sort of equipment (particularly communications equipment) to rule your life.

Don't be afraid to turn off telephones, television sets and computers. Make a real effort to use gadgets to improve your life – and reduce your workload.

And when you can feel yourself being pressurised into dealing with numerous apparently urgent and vital problems stop and ask yourself just how significant those problems will be in six months or six years time. That should help put the apparent urgency of those problems into perspective.

Just because the technology is available it doesn't necessarily follow that it is essential to use it – or, indeed, that it is or would be wise to use it.

Sometimes the simpler technologies are much better.

As I was writing this chapter I telephoned a friend who works in a very large organisation. She was out. The colleague who answered the telephone told me that he would leave a message on her computer.

'Exactly what do you mean by put a message on her computer?' I asked him.

'I'll scribble a note on a yellow sticky pad and put the note on her computer screen,' said the wise man.

95. I have learned to be always prepared to ask dumb sounding questions. You can't afford not to ask them. Asking dumb questions requires courage.

And I'm prepared to bet that when you ask the dumb sounding question other people around you will breathe a sigh of relief that you've asked the question they wanted to ask but didn't have the nerve.

96. I have learned how to bamboozle bureaucrats.

Bureaucrats are the true plague of the 21st century. Honoré de Balzac said that bureaucracy is a great machine operated by pigmies. Knowing how to deal with them effectively is vital. Here are two examples of simple ways in which you can deal with bureaucrats.

1. Use their own rules against them.
When I was a general practitioner a bureaucrat called to say that he would be collecting, and taking away, all the medical records in my possession. He said that he had to take them away to check for some inexplicable, incomprehensible but documented bureaucratic reason. (Bureaucrats always have inexplicable, incomprehensive but documented reasons for what they do). I told him that he couldn't take them away. I said I needed the medical records in order to treat my patients and that even if I didn't need the medical records I regarded them as confidential. The bureaucrat said if I looked at the bottom of each medical records envelope I would see that the medical records belonged to the Minister of Health and that he, as the Minister's representative, was therefore entitled to take the records with him. With a flash of inspiration I told him that he could take the medical records – but that he would have to leave the ink behind. 'The medical records may belong to the Minister,' I explained. 'But the ink is mine.' The bureaucrat thought about this for a while, consulted some colleagues and then went away and did not come back.

2. Remember – and use the fact – that bureaucrats are terrified of responsibility.
When patients move from one part of the country to another, and therefore from one practice to another their medical records follow them at a far more leisurely pace. It is not unknown for medical records to take several months to make a journey of just a few miles. If you allowed the medical records to make their own way they would probably get to their destination more speedily. On one occasion a new patient, a diabetic, needed treatment. I did not have her medical records. I telephoned her previous doctor. He could not remember anything useful about the patient's condition or treatment. But, he said, all the information I needed was on her medical records which he had dispatched to

his layer of bureaucrats some days earlier. I telephoned his bureaucrats. They told me that the medical records had been sent to my local bureaucrats. I telephoned my local bureaucrats. They agreed that they had the medical records in question. A bureaucrat confirmed that they were, as we spoke, sitting on her desk. I pointed out, politely, that I needed them urgently. The bureaucrat said that it would be another week or so before I could have them. I explained that the situation was rather more urgent than that. I said I would drive over to the bureaucrat's office to retrieve the medical records. The bureaucrat said I could not do that. I asked if I could drive over to examine the records without taking them away. The bureaucrat said I could not do that either. I then told the bureaucrat that if the medical records were not on my desk within thirty minutes, and the patient concerned died, I would put the bureaucrat down on the death certificate as a contributory cause of death. The medical records were on my desk within thirty minutes. The bureaucrat brought them in person by taxi. I had discovered the single most important truth about bureaucrats: they do not like responsibility. A vampire will recoil at the sign of the cross. A bureaucrat will recoil at the threat of responsibility.

97. I have learned that it is important to ignore (at least some of) the rules.

In any society there will always be people who like creating their own mini laws – called rules. As our society becomes increasingly complex (in many different ways) so there are more and more excuses for small–minded people to create new rules; many of which serve only to substantiate the power and influence of the people who create them. As Thoreau said, any fool can make a rule. And every fool will mind it.

Some rules are self–imposed. People create their own rules out of routine and tradition. When you ask people why they are doing something a particular way, you will often hear the answers: 'That's the way I was taught' or 'Because that's the way we do it.' Those are little more than excuses for avoiding thought. Most people are shackled and constrained by many invisible, non–existent, self–imposed beliefs and rules which they have created for themselves, or which they have allowed others to create for them.

Most rules come from bureaucrats. Bureaucrats love rules. In particular they love rules which enable them to say 'no'. Most local and central government departments now follow the Russian way of doing things: 'If we don't say you can do it then you can't do it.'

The waves of legislation are not going to stop crashing onto our shores.

Most of the most recent, and egregiously illogical, legislation which has affected our lives has come from Brussels, on behalf of the European Union.

You should not be afraid of ignoring, breaking or sidestepping the bureaucrat's rules (as long as you can do so without breaking the law, of course). If you can think of a new, different and possibly better way to do something then don't be afraid to try it. You may astound yourself and the rest of the world. Your own conscience should be the only rule maker you always obey. The only person you really have to be responsible to is yourself.

You might find it a revealing, enlightening and ultimately liberating exercise to make a list of all the rules which run your life. Include the rules which govern your personal life as well as those which run your business life.

When you have compiled your list write the question 'Why?' by each rule. And try to decide where all those rules originated. Many of the rules which still run your personal life will have doubtless originated with your parents and schoolteachers. Some will have originated with a previous employer. Some you will have absorbed, as though by osmosis, from friends. And many you will have acquired from 'Society'.

Every time you think of, or come across, another rule ask yourself whether the rule is essential or avoidable. Ask yourself whether the rule adds quality to your life. And ask yourself whether or not there are alternatives.

Many rules are designed to stop us doing things. Others simply convince us that we cannot do things, that we aren't good enough and that we are doomed to be poor and to fail if we do not satisfy certain preconceived conditions. What nonsense rules are.

Remember that there is no such thing as impossible. The impossible is merely the limit of your imagination. Modern scientists, invariably working for corporations and government sponsored research organisations, say that something is impossible when what they really mean is that they don't understand it and cannot explain it according to the existing rules – and that they are, therefore, more than a little frightened by it.

Don't allow yourself to be constrained by the rules – or by other people's views of what is or is not possible. You do not have to do things the way others do them. You can play the game of life by any rules you like. If you are going to get anywhere in life then ignoring at least some of the rules is almost a prerequisite.

The number of absurd rules and unhelpful regulations controlling our lives will continue to increase until or unless the European Union is disbanded.

98. I have learned that in order to banish my fears I must first know what I am afraid of.

A little fear is a good thing. Fear helps us stay alive.

I remember a skiing holiday I took a few years ago. I had only been skiing once before and was with a group of beginners but within minutes of arriving on the slopes for the first time I found myself standing at the top of an extremely steep and nasty looking slope.

Everyone in my group of novice skiers expressed alarm and fear. Our very young ski instructor laughed at us and told us that he knew no fear and that we should also have no fear. I (and the other members of my group) quickly abandoned him. I have a rule never to do anything potentially hazardous in the company of someone who does not know fear.

But not all fear is good, useful or welcome.

Fear is one of the most potent, all–pervasive and destructive forces in our society. Fear will stop you thinking and may interfere with the way you behave. Animals, who can smell fear, know that it is a sign of weakness.

Fear, worry and anxiety lead to fatigue and exhaustion and to mental, physical and spiritual illness. (The real paradox here is that a fear of illness can create illness).

It is because they fear what others will or might say that so many people make themselves ill with work in order to buy new and fashionable motor cars, clothes and gadgets they do not really need. Fear, together with indecision and doubt, is a major enemy of success.

Many people say, boldly and almost defiantly, that they fear nothing. They are either lying or deluding themselves. Everyone fears something. We fear anything which controls or handicaps us physically, spiritually or mentally.

Conquering your fears is a vital step on the road to liberating your spirit and reaching personal freedom. But before you can conquer your fears you must first know exactly what those fears are. You must examine yourself and analyse your fears. Fears which are not confronted will grow and grow and eventually destroy you.

Most modern human fears are created by the culture in which we live. Naturally, we are susceptible to the basic, commonplace fears which affect other members of the animal kingdom. We fear hunger and pain, for example. But we also fear sickness, poverty, imprisonment, lack of freedom, loneliness and unemployment. We fear cancer, financial ruin, secret exposure and jealousy. We fear losing love and we fear failure.

We even fear getting old.

Many who fear old age spend much of their time and money on trying to look younger than they are. Others simply apologise for their age and use it as an excuse for everything that others criticise. Those who are most conscious of the effects of age, and most worried about ageing, are, inevitably, the ones who are most likely to suffer the adverse effects of old age. The fear of old age inevitably also includes the fears of poverty, death, ill health and pain and a loss of financial and physical freedom and independence.

And yet the fear of old age can to a large extent be eliminated by accepting it as a blessing, by realising that you have understanding and wisdom that you didn't have when you were young.

We fear criticism, rejection and ridicule too. This type of fear is the basis of all kinds of modern fashions. When we buy our clothes, motor cars, jewellery and household furnishings we are conscious of the fact that if we choose the wrong items we may arouse the contempt of those around us. We are afraid that they will laugh at us if we buy the wrong things.

A fear of criticism robs a man of imagination, self–reliance and initiative. A fear of criticism is one of the main reasons why most people never move from their rut.

One of the commonest of all fears is that of poverty. Fear of poverty is a powerful and destructive state of mind which can destroy reason, self–reliance, imagination, enthusiasm, ambition and determination. We fear poverty because we know that few things bring as much suffering and humiliation. We fear poverty because we know that there are many cruel and rapacious individuals (and corporations) in the world who will take our money away from us without compunction – and others who will then take advantage of us and persecute us because of our poverty.

A fear of poverty often makes decision making difficult and deadens ambition; it creates pessimism and breeds doubts and excuses. Many people who worry about becoming poor spend a lot of their time planning what to do if a venture fails. They tend to procrastinate and be over cautious. And, not surprisingly, they are often also cautious about committing themselves to anything that might prove hazardous.

Our fear of poverty is enhanced by the fact that we are taught by our society that money is the key to all happiness.

Although it is undoubtedly true that money can buy some of the freedoms which lead to happiness, most people do not use money properly and certainly do not use it to buy freedom. On the contrary, most people do exactly the opposite – they give up their freedom to buy money and then spend the money they have acquired buying 'things' which imprison them in responsibilities.

Many people spend their lives afraid. They are afraid of illness, afraid of poverty, afraid of the boss, afraid of the doctor, afraid of work, afraid of their own shortcomings, afraid of mother, afraid of father, afraid of what the neighbours might think, afraid of not having any money, afraid of losing the money they do have, afraid of what strangers might say to one another about them, afraid of being unemployed and afraid of the police.

If it senses that you are afraid a dog will bark louder and be far more likely to bite. People are much the same. If you walk down the street timidly, showing fear, then the chances are much higher that you will be accosted or mugged. If you show fear then the children or youths you pass will be more likely to gather around and sneer and mock. Show fear and the hunt will be on.

Most people never do anything with their lives because they spend every day worrying and thinking and scheming about what has already happened (and about which they can do nothing) and what might happen (about which they can also do nothing).

They spend days and weeks and months and years rewriting history in their minds – or (and just as futile) trying to write a script for the future or to predict what will happen to them in one, five or ten years time. Far too much energy and effort is wasted worrying about what might go wrong and what other people will think if something does go wrong, and what the authorities might or might not do.

When you are worried about something ask yourself how much it really matters.

Does it really matter very much if your car has a scratch down the side or if you are seen in clothes which are not at the height of fashion? Does it really matter very much if you have to go out with a hole in your stocking? Is the world going to stop revolving if you make a bad speech? Will your business collapse if you go away for a few days?

In order to defeat your secret inner fears you must analyse them, find out what is behind them, bring them out into the open, confront them, look at them from every possible angle, examine them in detail, make them look silly and humiliate them.

You must always look at the bottom line to find out how much harm these hidden, secret fears can really do to you. What is the worst that can happen to you if such and such a fear comes to fruition? Facing and confronting the bottom line can be a powerful way to disembowel a fear, an anxiety or a worry.

What is the worst that can happen? Would the worst really be so bad?

Finally, find yourself a passion and a purpose that transcends ordinary life and you will find it much easier to forget the day to day problems which are otherwise likely to cause you so much distress. You will only achieve true freedom of your spirit when your life is full and you aren't frightened of anything or anyone.

99. I have learned that it is important to minimise the amount of fat I eat.

If I eat too much fatty food there is a risk that my body's white cells – crucial warriors in my body's immune system defences – may be damaged. And if I have lots of fat in my blood that will also affect my body's ability to deal with infections.

In a normal, healthy body white cells constantly patrol the blood stream hunting out bacteria (and stray cancer cells). If the blood stream is clogged with fat the white cells simply cannot move around effectively.

Imagine how difficult it would be for a group of lifeguards to swim through an oil slick and you'll have an idea of just how difficult it is for white cells to move through fat soaked blood.

Incidentally, all fats are bad for your immune system – but animal fats are probably worse than others and can probably do more damage to your immune system. One of the reasons for this is the fact that animal fat is often contaminated with chemical residues – toxic and possibly carcinogenic residues of drugs consumed (accidentally or deliberately) by feeding animals.

Governments often recommend that a healthy diet should contain no more than 30% fat. I think that figure is far too high (probably because a relatively high fat diet helps keep the food industry rich and happy). I believe that you should aim to have no more than 15–20% fat in your diet. If for some reason you need to follow a low fat diet you may wish to cut your consumption of fat to 10–15%. (There is more about fat – and other foodstuffs – in my book *Food for Thought*.)

To calculate the percentage of fat in foods look at the calorie list on the package label and divide the number of calories obtained from fat by the total number of calories; then multiply that total by 100 to obtain the percentage.

100. I have learned that whenever I find myself facing a problem the answer is to focus on the solution rather than the problem.

101. I have learned that I am the best investment I'll ever make.

You are the best investment you'll ever make too. Invest in your education (formal or informal). Put as much time as you can into improving your knowledge. Remember that imagination and a capacity for hard work are far more important than formal qualifications. And if you have a good business idea, and you have a little capital, doesn't it make sense to invest in yourself? Put your own money into your business and you will retain control. Allow banks or investors to put up all the money and they will take over. If your business becomes successful, they will be the ones to profit.

Never forget your roots. And never forget how you became the person you are. You never know, you might have to do it all again.

And, remember, it isn't money that matters.

Money is just money. In the end the lawyers and the taxmen get it all anyway.

The Extras

There are no 'right' or 'wrong' answers. Only *your* answers.

Extra 1

Questions To Make You Think

Most of us go through our lives in a rush. As a result many important things happen by chance.

We spend days and weeks worrying over small problems (such as which car to buy) but never find time to ponder big questions (how do I really want to spend the rest of my life?).

We never have time to stop and think about who we are, what we do or where our lives are heading.

So take a little time today to answer these questions.

You may find that in doing so you learn a bit more about yourself – and a little more about who you are and where you're heading.

1. Take away your family, your job, your home and your money. What is left?
2. What in your life gives you the most stress and the most grief? What makes you miserable? What can you do to have less of that in your life?
3. What in your life gives you the most pleasure? What can you do to get more of it?
4. Which individuals do you most admire? Why? How could you change your life to match their ideals?
5. How could you best improve your life?
6. What are the three most important lessons you have learned in your life? (Imagine you are dying and you want to pass on your greatest learning. What would you say?)
7. If you could give the world just one Commandment what would it be? (The Vernon Coleman special for the day is: 'Thou shalt be kind.')
8. If you had all the money you needed what would you do?
9. If you found out you had 10 years to live, in your present state of health, what would you do differently?

10. If you found out you had one year to live, in your present state of health, what would you do differently?

11. If you had 24 hours to live what would you regret not having done or tried?

12. Is anything too serious for jokes? If so, what?

13. You find that your best friend has stolen money to pay for medical treatment for a seriously ill relative. What would you do?

14. How much have you controlled the course your life has taken?

15. A dear friend is in agony and wants you to help him/her to die. Would you?

16. What would you do if your country started a war which you considered unjustified?

17. You see three teenagers making fun of a mentally handicapped man in the street. What would you do?

18. Has your life ever been changed by an apparently random occurrence?

19. Do you find it easy to ask for help?

20. You're having dinner with people you respect and admire. They all criticise a close friend of yours (not knowing he/she is a friend). The criticism is unjustified. What would you do?

Extra 2

The Best Self Help Books For Inspiration And Spiritual Guidance

It is considered quite good sport these days for newspaper and television commentators to mock self–help books – suggesting that the people who write them are exploitative, and that the people who read them are rather sad. This is a pity because, over the years, books of all kinds have provided millions of stressed, fearful, lonely individuals with an enormous amount of comfort and courage.

True, it's a pity that there is a need for such books. But the need for books offering guidance and support has risen for two very simple reasons.

First, although it sounds strange to admit it, we live in possibly the most stressful period man has ever known. Most of us have enough to eat and most of us have warm, dry shelter. Our basic problems have been solved. But, the pace and confusion of our modern world means that stress related disorders (affecting the body, the mind and the soul) are commoner than ever before. Second, just when we all need all the support we can get we find we are more on our own than ever before in history. For most of us the comforting, all embracing family is now a thing of the past. It is easier to travel than ever before in history, and communication networks are faster and (theoretically at least) more effective than at any other time in history, and yet most people spend an increasing part of their lives miles away from the people who are most likely to give them the succour (and the advice) they need. Although we may communicate with one another speedily and frequently how often do we say anything really worth saying? For example, at a guess I would say that 99.99% of all e–mails are little more than electronic froth; superficial and insignificant.

Today we all need all the help and guidance we can get. And if we can pick up a tip or a trick or a thought that will help us along the stony road of life what on earth is wrong with that? We need help in finding a new path to follow; we need help in finding a purpose, a righteous passion and an aim which involves a little more and goes a little higher than double glazing and 56 channel satellite television.

Some of the books on my list may surprise you. But these are, I believe, books that are all well worth reading. Some may change the way you look at your problems. One or two may change your life. Most are beautifully written, often poetic, and also full of sincerity and wisdom. There are thousands of other books in my library which didn't make this list but which are equally deserving of a place on it. (There are, for example, no novels on this list). But a list always has to have a beginning and an end. At least, it does if it's going to fit into a book.

Incidentally, although for simplicity I have put the books in a numbered list, there is no significance to the placing of titles on the list. All these books are well worth reading.

1. Walden, or Life in the Woods and Civil Disobedience – Henry David Thoreau
All Thoreau's books are packed with simple, scorching wisdom. Thoreau was a real revolutionary.

2. Tao te Ching – Lao Tsu
Often simply known as the 'Lao Tsu' this is the main classic in Tao thinking. Although it is usually described as having been written by Lao Tsu (who was an older contemporary of Confucius) this book is probably an anthology of wise sayings edited, rather than written, by the 'author'.

3. The Penguin Book of Twentieth Century Protest – edited by Brian MacArthur
A fine, inspirational and invaluable collection of articles, speeches, extracts, essays and heaven knows what else, written by people protesting and complaining about everything under the sun – but doing it always with style, honesty, determination and passion.

4. Self–Help – Samuel Smiles
Samuel Smiles was the original, modern 'self–help' guru. His remarkably uplifting book *Self–Help* was written in 1859 and became one of the most successful non–fiction books of the late 19th century. Today the book is largely forgotten (and, when remembered, derided) but its message is as valid now as it ever was.

5. *The Conquest of Happiness* – Bertrand Russell

Russell describes his brand of wisdom as common sense. But whatever else it is, common sense certainly isn't common. Russell's own appetite for life is legendary and this provocative, idiosyncratic and iconoclastic book (which is surprisingly little known) reflects his own joy in taking life by the scruff of the neck.

6. *The Prince* – Niccolo Macchiaveli

The original treatise on statecraft contains more raw wisdom per inch than a year of television chat shows can offer their blanched and unblinking viewers.

7. *Small is Beautiful* – E. F. Schumacher

Once very much in fashion Schumacher's concept is now almost forgotten (and, when it is remembered often reviled) in a world where Big is Powerful. Schumacher challenged traditional doctrines, put the emphasis on people not products or profits and argued that Capital should serve Man instead of the other way round.

8. *The Power Of Positive Thinking* – Norman Vincent Peale

First published in 1953, now a classic that is nevertheless often overlooked and ignored. Infinitely better than thousands of the 'me–too' books which have offered pretty much the same advice.

9. *How To Win Friends and Influence People* – Dale Carnegie

Another book that is easily forgotten among the mass of talk show generated and publicised self–help books now pouring out of America. But this massive international best–seller is still valid and if you've never read it you will, I think, find it hugely rewarding. Carnegie was a master at using anecdotes to illustrate his themes. Simplistic in places the book is nevertheless just as readable as a good novel.

10. *Wind, Sand and Stars* – Antoine d'Exupery

A haunting, beautiful, brave, often sad, book written in blood by the author of the exquisite classic *The Little Prince*.

11. *'The Outsider'* – Colin Wilson

When first published in 1956 this book was received with great applause and enthusiasm. Wilson was lionised. *The Outsider* is still seminal reading for anyone interested in the human mind, creativity and individuality.

12. *The Road To Serfdom* – F. A. Hayek

The essential modern work on liberty. Hayek's short book about freedom in our society should be compulsory reading. No one should be allowed to leave school without having read it at least once, and preferably twice. I would far rather students understood Hayek's thesis than that they grasped the principles of algebra.

13. The Autobiography of Mark Twain – Edited by Charles Neider
I deliberately haven't filled this list with biographies and autobiographies (though I could think of scores which are truly inspirational) but Mark Twain's is a true classic and reeks of Twain's unique approach to life: full of gentle humour and unbridled imagination and written with great style. Read this book and you will feel that you really know the man and his life. Twain describes the good, the bad and the ugly with the same even handed approach and the book is full of tragedy, drama, humour and great wisdom.

14. Meditations of a Solitary Walker – Jean–Jaques Rousseau
Rousseau was alienated, philosophical, isolated and sometimes more than slightly paranoid. But his meditations provide an excellent guide book through our complex and often unjust society.

15. Essays – Ralph Waldo Emerson
Civilised, gentle and constantly wise, Emerson's style isn't always easy to read, but what he has to say is invariably worth the effort. An idealist, a rationalist, a transcendentalist and a determined advocate of spiritual independence.

16. Thus Spake Zarathustra – Friedrich Nietzsche
Philosophy, writer, scholar – how does anyone define Nietzsche? Born in Germany he became Swiss and was resolutely unconventional and individual. In his book Ecce Homo Nietzsche predicted that the 20th century would be a century of 'wars such as have never happened on earth' because human beings would no longer have a god to turn to, to absolve them of their guilt. Humans would, he forecast, be racked by their unfocussed guilt and would turn the blind and reassuring faith with which they had formerly worshipped their God into an equally unblinking belief in barbaric, nationalistic brotherhoods. Nietzsche said that man would limp through the 20th century but that the 21st century would be more dreadful still for there would be a 'total eclipse of all values'.

17. Illusions: The Adventures of a Reluctant Messiah – Richard Bach
Best known as the author of Jonathan Livingston Seagull, Richard Bach is one of the very best and most imaginative inspirational writers of the 20th century.

18. The Anatomy Of An Illness – Norman Cousins
An inspirational, triumphant modern classic in which Cousins describes how he took a share in the responsibility for overcoming a crippling and supposedly irreversible disease. Cousins is famous for having proved that laughter can cure but this book offers far more than that. It should be read and re–read by anyone who has a chronic illness, by all doctors and nurses and by anyone nursing a patient with a chronic or threatening illness.

19. An Inland Voyage – Robert Louis Stevenson
Describes a canoe tour in Belgium and Northern France but is much more than just a travel book. The journey took place in the same year as the tour which led to the better known book *Travels with a Donkey in the Cevennes*. Written when he was 28 this book came long before *Treasure Island, Kidnapped* and *The Strange Case of Dr Jekyll and Mr Hyde* made Stevenson famous.

20. The Art of War – Sun Tzu
The Art of War is one of the most remarkable books ever written. It was written in China 2,500 years ago and there is no doubt that if our own leaders would read the book we would all be safer and less vulnerable. At least one expert has argued that if our 20th century leaders had read (and followed) this book World Wars I and II could have been avoided, the British Empire would not have been dismembered and the wars in Vietnam and Korea would not have been the disaster they were.

Napoleon read it and used *The Art of War*. It is believed that the book (which was not translated into English until 1905 but which had been available in a French edition since 1782) was Napoleon's secret weapon and his key to success.

There is no doubt that Napoleon used Sun Tzu's principles to great advantage and it was only when he failed to follow Sun Tzu's rules of engagement that he was finally defeated.

But the advice in *The Art of War* does not only apply to warriors engaged in traditional forms of warfare.The advice applies equally well in many other forms of combat and confrontation. Look closely and you will see how some modern leaders have used the advice it contains.

Extra 3

The Author

Vernon Coleman was an angry young man for as long as it was decently possible. He then turned into an angry middle–aged man. And now, with no effort whatsoever, he has matured into being an angry old man. He is, he confesses, just as angry as he ever was. Indeed, he may be even angrier because, he says, the more he learns about life the more things he finds to be angry about.

Cruelty, prejudice and injustice are the three things most likely to arouse his well–developed sense of ire but he admits that, at a pinch, inefficiency, incompetence and greed will do almost as well. He does not cope well with bossy people, particularly when they are dressed in uniform and attempting to confiscate his Swiss Army penknife. 'Being told I can't do something has always seemed to me sufficient reason to do it,' he says. 'And being told that I must do something has always seemed to me a very good reason not to do it.'

The author has an innate dislike of taking orders, a pathological contempt for pomposity, hypocrisy and the sort of unthinking political correctness which attracts support from Guardian reading pseudo–intellectuals. He also has a passionate loathing for those in authority who do not understand that unless their authority is tempered with compassion and a sense of responsibility the end result must always be an extremely unpleasant brand of totalitarianism.

Vernon Coleman has written for *The Guardian, Daily Telegraph, Sunday Telegraph, Observer, Sunday Times, Daily Mail, Mail on Sunday, Daily Express, Sunday Express, Daily Star, The Sun, News of the World, Daily Mirror, Sunday Mirror, The People, Woman, Woman's Own, Spectator, Punch, The Lady* and hundreds of other leading publications in Britain and around the world. His books have been published by Pan, Penguin, Corgi, Arrow and many other publishers in the UK and reproduced by scores of discerning publishers around the world.

He has never had a proper job (in the sense of working for someone else in regular, paid employment with a cheque or pay packet at the end of a week or month) but he has had freelance and temporary employment in many forms. He has, for example, had paid employment as: magician's assistant, postman, fish delivery van driver, production line worker, chemical laboratory assistant, author, publisher, draughtsman, meals on wheels driver, feature writer, drama critic, book reviewer, columnist, surgeon, police surgeon, industrial medical officer, social worker, night club operator, property developer, magazine editor, general practitioner, private doctor, television presenter, radio presenter, agony aunt, university lecturer, casualty doctor and care home assistant.

Today, he likes books, films, cafes and writing. He has never been much of an athlete, though he once won a certificate for swimming a width of the public baths in Walsall (which was, at the time, in Staffordshire but has now, apparently, been moved elsewhere).

He doesn't like yappy dogs, big snarly dogs with saliva dripping from their fangs or people who think that wearing a uniform automatically gives them status and rights. He likes trains, dislikes planes and used to like cars until some idiot invented speed cameras, bus lanes and car parks where the spaces are so narrow that only the slimmest of vehicles will fit in.

He is fond of cats, pens and notebooks and used to like watching cricket until the authorities sold out and allowed people to paint slogans on the grass. His interests and hobbies include animals, books, photography, drawing, chess, backgammon, cinema, philately, billiards, sitting in cafes and on benches and collecting Napoleana. He likes log fires and bonfires, motor racing and music by Mahler and dislikes politicians, bureaucrats and cauliflower cheese. He likes videos but loathes DVDs. His favourite people in history include Napoleon

Bonaparte, W.G. Grace, William Cobbett, P.G.Wodehouse, Jerome K. Jerome, and Walter Raleigh all of whom had more than it takes and most of whom were English. (Napoleon would have been if he'd had the chance.)

He lives in the village of Bilbury in Devon and enjoys malt whisky, toasted muffins and old films. He is devoted to Donna Antoinette who is the kindest, sweetest, most sensitive woman a man could hope to meet and who, as an undeserved but welcome bonus, makes the very best roast parsnips on the planet.

For a catalogue of Vernon Coleman's books please write to:

Publishing House
Trinity Place
Barnstaple
Devon EX32 9HG
England

Telephone   01271 328892
Fax   01271 328768

Outside the UK:
Telephone   +44 1271 328892
Fax   +44 1271 328768

Or visit our website:
www.vernoncoleman.com

Moneypower

'Tactics and Strategies for the Thinking Investor'

"Vernon Coleman promises to reveal the secrets of power over money and this is exactly what he delivers in this excellent book. Split into three main sections, Vernon initially explains a variety of practical methods for keeping your money, and the detrimental effects of emotional spending.

Section 2 provides honest and straightforward advice on the nuts and bolts of investing, and section 3 explains Vernon's 100 Laws of Money.

This is a very honest and upfront book. It is very clear that Vernon has many years experience investing his own money. The fact that he feels qualified to write such a book suggests he has been very successful. However, his investment mistakes are fully explained so you won't need to repeat them.

I have read (and loved) The Richest Man In Babylon and am a big fan of investment guru Warren Buffett and am a qualified financial advisor. To my surprise I learnt a lot from this book and cannot recommend it enough.

For me the section on dividends (pages 92-95) is worth the purchase price alone!

As with all quality books don't just read it, but use it. You will never look back." (AMAZON FIVE STAR REVIEW)

Published in hardback by Blue Books price £19.99

How To Stop Your Doctor Killing You

Dr Coleman has been a passionate advocate of patients' rights for over thirty years, and in writing this book he has drawn together a vast amount of information which will help readers to live longer and healthier lives. It shows how patients can protect themselves against an increasingly incompetent and dangerous medical profession.

Topics covered include:
- Don't let your doctor bully you
- How to survive in hospital
- The real cause of cancer – and the solution
- How to manipulate your doctor
- Tests and investigations – are they safe?
- Should you get a second opinion?
- Questions to ask your surgeon
- Ten good reasons why you shouldn't trust your doctor

Published in paperback by European Medical Journal price £12.99

Order from Publishing House • Trinity Place • Barnstaple • Devon EX32 9HG • England
Telephone 01271 328892 • Fax 01271 328768
or order online from www.vernoncoleman.com

Oil Apocalypse

How to Survive, Protect Your Family And Profit Through The Coming Years of Crisis

Why the oil apocalypse is inevitable. How and why our dependence on oil will end in tears. And how you can prepare yourself and your family. Also includes

- Our unhealthy addiction to a gift of nature
- Peak oil: the beginning of the end of civilisation
- What will happen when the oil runs out
- Your personal survival plan
- Investing to survive the oil apocalypse

'I am writing to offer my sincere congratulations on such a well researched book. It made fascinating reading and personally I accept your frightening prognosis...I write as one who...spent several years working in the...oil and gas industry.' (R.W. Sussex)

'...the most disturbing and enlightening book I have ever read. No book has ever had such a profound effect on me.' (M.C., Sheffield)

'Intense reading. Coleman's message is blunt and this book will frighten you, but bury your head in the sand at your own peril. If you don't believe him then keep an eye on the price at the pump.' (Geoffrey Taylor, Shropshire Star)

'Generally I don't subscribe to doom mongers books. But I read *Oil Apocalypse* this weekend and it was terrific. Very insightful. Brilliant book.' (J.S., by e-mail)

Published in paperback by Blue Books price £12.99

Superbody

A healthy immune system doesn't just protect you against infection – it is an essential factor in your body's ability to fight off all other diseases – including cancer.

The first two parts of this book explain why and how our bodies are under siege – and why the incidence of cancer and infectious diseases is rising rapidly (and likely to continue rising).

Infectious diseases started to become resistant to antibiotics a quarter of a century ago. Since then the situation has steadily worsened and it is now probably too late for the medical profession to reverse the situation. Infectious diseases are coming back in a big way and the incidence of cancer is also going to continue to rise.

And so the third part of Superbody explains how you can protect yourself against these, and other threats, by improving the strength, efficiency and effectiveness of your immune system.

Published in paperback by European Medical Journal price £9.99

Order from Publishing House • Trinity Place • Barnstaple • Devon EX32 9HG • England
Telephone 01271 328892 • Fax 01271 328768 • www.vernoncoleman.com

How To Protect And Preserve Your Freedom, Identity And Privacy

Thousands of people fall victim to identity theft every year. The consequences can be devastating and can take years to sort out.

Banks and Government departments take poor care of the vital, private information they demand. It's hardly surprising that identity theft is the fastest growing crime in the world.

There are scores of ways that your identity can be stolen. The majority of people aren't aware of just how vulnerable they are until it's too late.

How To Protect And Preserve Your Freedom, Identity And Privacy gives advice on:

* What to do if you're a victim of identity theft.
* The type of phone that can protect you against fraud.
* The tricks fraudsters use at cash machines.
* The signs which show that your identity may have been stolen.
* What to watch out for when using your credit card in shops and restaurants.
* How to protect your security before you go on holiday.
* Why you should be wary of the 'postman' knocking at your door – and the e-mails you should be frightened of.
* How answering your phone could leave you vulnerable to fraud.
* Why you should be wary about the clothes you wear and much, much more.

Vernon Coleman's best-seller contains crucial security tips for personal survival in the 21st century.

Published in paperback by Blue Books, price £9.99

How To Live Longer

Dr Coleman has always argued that every individual should have the right to take control of his or her own health.

You should make the decisions about what happens to you. You should not allow anyone to make vital decisions for you. Doctors make mistakes and most have a vested interest of some kind.

How To Live Longer is packed with information and advice and the aim of the book is simply to enable you to make better decisions about your own health and health care – and about how to live longer and how to stay healthier and as 'young' as possible.

Published in paperback by European Medical Journal price £12.99

Order from Publishing House • Trinity Place • Barnstaple • Devon EX32 9HG • England
Telephone 01271 328892 • Fax 01271 328768 • www.vernoncoleman.com

Coleman's Laws

"However good your doctor is – and however much you may trust him or her – you must share the responsibility for your own health, and you must know when to tell your doctor if you think that the treatment with which he or she is providing you could be causing problems.

After all, your nice friendly doctor is far more likely to kill you than is a burglar, a deranged relative or a drunken motorist.

Sadly, things aren't going to get any better. Medicine is becoming ever more complex by the day, and medical students and young nurses are being taught within a system which is geared towards defending administrators and drug companies. In many hospitals patients are regarded (if they are regarded at all) as a nuisance. And things will only change for the better when patients and the honest professionals who do care are prepared to stand up and make their voices heard.

I have built this book around twelve basic laws of medicine which I have, over the years, formulated for my own benefit, as a doctor, an observer and a patient. I have illustrated the twelve laws with clinical anecdotes and scientific data."

Published in paperback by the European Medical Journal priced £12.99

Health Secrets Doctors Share With Their Families

written with Donna Antoinette Coleman

A guide to health tips and treatments which you can apply at home – and which really work. It's a complete A to Z of caring; a pocket encyclopaedia written to help keep you and your family healthy and to help you cure day to day health problems.

The tips, advice and suggestions have been collected over many years and are a result of thousands of conversations with doctors, nurses, osteopaths, acupuncturists, herbalists and other health professionals and of correspondence with tens of thousands of experts and readers. Packed with tips, remedies and practical advice on staying healthy and dealing with health problems.

Published in paperback by the European Medical Journal priced £12.99

"Packed with invaluable advice on everything from acne to zoster via brittle nails and snoring. I love the way everything is explained in language you don't need a degree in rocket science to understand. It's timeless and more valuable than a first aid kit." (Mrs T.P., Notts)

"...a most useful and informative commonsense reference book." (R.W., Sussex)

Order from Publishing House • Trinity Place • Barnstaple • Devon EX32 9HG • England
Telephone 01271 328892 • Fax 01271 328768
or order online from www.vernoncoleman.com

Bodypower

It may sound too good to be true. But it is true. There is a free, doctor-approved secret with which you can, for the rest of your life, easily conquer 9 out of 10 illnesses without spending money or seeing a doctor.

When you have 'Bodypower', most illnesses can be conquered without pills or medicines and without orthodox or alternative therapies.

You can get better without spending time and money on doctors, specialists, acupuncturists, hypnotherapists or pills from the chemist – and without exposing yourself to hazardous and uncomfortable side effects.

As a bonus, Bodypower includes simple but effective tips on: How to stay slim for life – How to improve your figure – How to break bad habits – How to relax your body and mind – and much, much more.

Published in paperback by the European Medical Journal priced £9.99

Mindpower

Nothing has the potential to influence your health quite as much as your mind. Most doctors around the world now agree that at least 75% of all illnesses can be caused or made worse by stress and anxiety. But although your mind can make you ill, it also has an enormous capacity to heal and cure. *Mindpower* will show you how to use your extraordinary natural, mental powers to improve your health.

Published in paperback by the European Medical Journal priced £12.99

Spiritpower

We are all composed of three parts: body, mind and spirit.

In *Bodypower*, Vernon Coleman describes the body's astonishing self-healing powers and explains how you can take advantage of those powers to stay healthy and to defeat 9 out of 10 physical illnesses. In the sequel *Mindpower* Vernon Coleman explores the powers of the mind, describes how you can harness positive emotions and conquer destructive emotions and explains how you can use your mind to heal your body and teach yourself mental self-defence.

In *Spiritpower*, he deals with the third, and most abstract of the "body, mind, spirit" trilogy. He explores the essential elements of a healthy spirit by examining liberty and personal freedom in the twenty-first century.

This is a timely book which is sure to be met with as much enthusiasm as the first two publications in this trilogy of titles. It examines the reasons for our loss of freedom and personal dignity and describes how we can all regain our physical, mental and spiritual freedom.

Published in paperback by the European Medical Journal priced £12.99

Order from Publishing House • Trinity Place • Barnstaple • Devon EX32 9HG • England
Telephone 01271 328892 • Fax 01271 328768
or order online from www.vernoncoleman.com

Food for Thought

In his best-selling book Food for Thought Dr Coleman explains which foods are known to be associated with a wide range of diseases including: Asthma – Gall Bladder Disease – Headaches – Heart Trouble – High Blood Pressure – Indigestion – and many more. The book gives simple guidelines for healthy eating, lists 101 "superfoods" that can improve your health and offers simple, easy-to-follow slimming tips that can help you to lose weight permanently.

Published in paperback by the European Medical Journal priced £12.99

"Have just finished reading your latest edition of *Food for Thought*. I have found the book fascinating and informative and it has re-inforced many of my own views about how we are collectively being poisoned by what we ingest. I consider it to be one of the most brilliant books of its kind that I have ever read. Not only are the contents a mine of information and advice but the style is such that it makes the whole so thoroughly enjoyable to read; indeed it is a book difficult to put down" (G.P., London)

" I thought you might like to know that since receiving your book *Food For Thought* ... and acting on the advice given I have lost 7lbs and had a dramatic drop in blood pressure." (P.W., by email)

People Watching

If you would like to understand and get along with people better, find out how to make them like you and learn how to persuade them to do what you want, then you need People Watching.

In this amazing, informative and entertaining book Dr Vernon Coleman explains the subtle art of understanding body language, gestures, habits, clothing and other hidden clues. He explains what signals to look out for and what signals you should be putting out if you want to make the most out of what life has to offer.

Published in paperback by the Blue Books priced £9.99

"The ubiquitous media doc has done it yet again; this time turning his talents for producing sparkling gems of information in rapid-fire sequence to the field of body language and private habits. As always, he makes his subject both personally relevant and of practical use. Here's how to judge people by the bags they carry or the cars they drive, plus how to manipulate your doctor, appear sexy or make a rival uneasy, and a host of other tips too. Once you start to browse you would have to be a hermit not to find it unputdownable."
(The Good Book Guide)

Order from Publishing House • Trinity Place • Barnstaple • Devon EX32 9HG • England
Telephone 01271 328892 • Fax 01271 328768
or order online from www.vernoncoleman.com

Other books by Vernon Coleman

How To Conquer Health Problems Between Ages 50 and 120

written with Donna Antoinette Coleman

This book is a series of private consultations dealing with the diseases which cause most concern to the over 50s. Unlike most medical reference books this one is specifically written with the older reader in mind.

In addition to being packed with advice and practical tips How To Conquer Health Problems Between Ages 50 and 120 explains when you need to see a doctor (or alternative practitioner), what to ask and what to expect. Everything from Alzheimer's to wind is included and there are extensive sections dealing with arthritis, cancer, heart disease, IBS, maturity onset diabetes, osteoporosis, prostate disease and stroke. Here you will learn the truth about the treatments that work and those that don't.

Published in paperback by the European Medical Journal priced £15.99

All books available from:

Publishing House
Trinity Place
Barnstaple
Devon EX32 9HG
England

Telephone   01271 328892
Fax   01271 328768

Outside the UK:
Telephone   +44 1271 328892
Fax   +44 1271 328768

Or order from our website shop on:
www.vernoncoleman.com